The Ordinary Path to Holiness

R. THOMAS RICHARD, Ph.D.

Introduction by
Fr. Benedict Groeschel, CFR

ST PAULS

All Scripture references, unless otherwise noted, are taken from The New Testament: St. Paul Catholic Edition, © copyright 2000 by the Society of St. Paul, the Christian Community Bible (CCB), © copyright 1988 by St. Paul Publications, or the Revised Standard Version, Catholic Edition, © copyright 1965 (NT) and 1966 (OT) by Division of Christian Education of the National Council of the Churches of Christ in the United States of America.

Library of Congress Cataloging-in-Publication Data

Richard, R. Thomas.
   The ordinary path to holiness / R. Thomas Richard; introduction by Benedict Groeschel.
     p. cm.
     ISBN 0-8189-0913-7
     1. Spiritual life—Catholic Church.   I. Title.

   BX2350.65 .R53 2002
   246.4'82—dc21

                          2001056059

Nihil obstat
William J. O'Rourke
Censor Librorum

Imprimatur
✠ Daniel A. Hart
Bishop of Norwich
January 20, 1999

The *Nihil obstat* and *Imprimatur* are a declaration that a book or pamphlet is considered to be free from doctrinal and moral error. It is not implied that those who have granted the *Nihil obstat* and *Imprimatur* agree with the contents, opinions or statements expressed.

Produced and designed in the United States of America by the Fathers and Brothers of the Society of St. Paul, 2187 Victory Boulevard, Staten Island, New York 10314-6603, as part of their communications apostolate.

ISBN: 0-8189-0913-7

Printing Information:

Current Printing - first digit   1   2   3   4   5   6   7   8   9   10

Year of Current Printing - first year shown

2003   2004   2005   2006   2007   2008   2009   2010   2011   2012

The Ordinary Path to Holiness
is dedicated
to every person on the journey,
and is offered on their behalf
to our Father.

May He in His great mercy
bless this work,
and give grace to those
who, in their search for understanding,
take it up and use it.

This work is offered to Him
in union with my wife
Deborah,
and with much appreciation
for her help and encouragement.

TABLE OF CONTENTS

INTRODUCTION

When Dr. Thomas Richard first shared his book with me I was puzzled by the title. How can there be an ordinary path to an extraordinary state of being — holiness? As I read this remarkable little book over I realized precisely what he meant by *ordinary*, namely that path to God that is open and available to people in ordinary circumstances — lay people, active religious, parish priests. The paradox is that those who have callings outside these typical vocations — for instance, contemplative religious, monks, friars and lay people who are in unusual callings — all of these may be very ordinary people themselves.

I realized as I studied Dr. Richard's book that his choice of the word *ordinary* was meant to welcome those in ordinary vocations who are responding to the call of divine grace to a serious consideration of the journey toward God. Having studied and then preached and written about the spiritual journey for over fifty years I was more than interested. I was intrigued how a person in an *ordinary* vocation could present this familiar material to other *ordinary* people. He has done it very well.

The unique quality of this book is not its basic content. The spiritual journey is a topic that people have been discussing since St. Augustine and even before. The thing that makes this book particularly helpful is that it is written by a very well informed Christian layman who knows how lay people think and feel at this beginning of the Third Millennium. Being director of lay ministry formation for a whole diocese has given Dr. Richard an invaluable opportunity to develop his own ideas in this traditional area of thought. A similar and very popular effort to describe the spiritual life was made by M. Scott Peck in *The Road Less Traveled* (New York: Simon & Schuster, 1978). That book was written for those whose beliefs might not be explicitly founded on the Gospel but who had spiritual inclinations and were familiar with contemporary psychology. I also made an attempt to explore the spiritual journey in *Spiritual Passages* (New York: Crossroad, 1983) using insights drawn from the vast library of Catholic spiritual writers and from psychoanalytic theory. While not ignoring the psychological approach, Dr. Richard has emphasized theological concepts and spiritual doctrines more familiar to the well-read Christian reader. In fact, his book is specifically Catholic. By focusing on an audience who cherish the Mass, the sacraments and traditional Catholic teaching on the uses of suffering in union with Christ, Dr. Richard has been able to more profoundly explore these essentials of spiritual teaching. Like almost all books on the spiritual journey, this work is several books at one time.

Distinct topics like prayer and the sacraments are fitted in a helpful way to the needs of the spiritual traveler. An insightful discussion of the teachings of St. Teresa of Avila is included and helpfully related to the Lord's Prayer. Dr. Richard also traces the steps of the spiritual journey in various New Testament texts attempting, as others have done, to identify the stages of the spiritual journey in Scripture. Since operations of grace and the Holy Spirit are unique to each soul, these ideas should be seen as a fruitful source for meditation rather than as precise interpretations of the Bible.

The purpose of this book is practical — to help the serious Christian grow in the life of grace and to make progress on the journey Our Savior spoke of when He challenged His disciples, "Follow me!" This is a book not to be taken lightly. It does not call for speed-reading. Take your pencil and your time. Go back over things and meditate on various points. If you usually avoid marking up books so that you can pass them along to others, purchase two copies, one for your own serious study and one for lending out. This is a book to be chewed and digested. Any effort you make to understand the spiritual life will be amply rewarded because it will remain with you on your journey. If you read something you don't fully understand, come back to it later.

This is one of those rare books that is to be lived as well as read. But read it with your soul as well as your mind and with your heart as well as your eyes.

Fr. Benedict J. Groeschel, CFR
Author of *Spiritual Passages* and
The Journey Toward God

Biblical Abbreviations

OLD TESTAMENT

Genesis	Gn	Nehemiah	Ne	Baruch	Ba
Exodus	Ex	Tobit	Tb	Ezekiel	Ezk
Leviticus	Lv	Judith	Jdt	Daniel	Dn
Numbers	Nb	Esther	Est	Hosea	Ho
Deuteronomy	Dt	1 Maccabees	1 M	Joel	Jl
Joshua	Jos	2 Maccabees	2 M	Amos	Am
Judges	Jg	Job	Jb	Obadiah	Ob
Ruth	Rt	Psalms	Ps	Jonah	Jon
1 Samuel	1 S	Proverbs	Pr	Micah	Mi
2 Samuel	2 S	Ecclesiastes	Ec	Nahum	Na
1 Kings	1 K	Song of Songs	Sg	Habakkuk	Hab
2 Kings	2 K	Wisdom	Ws	Zephaniah	Zp
1 Chronicles	1 Ch	Sirach	Si	Haggai	Hg
2 Chronicles	2 Ch	Isaiah	Is	Malachi	Ml
Ezra	Ezr	Jeremiah	Jr	Zechariah	Zc
		Lamentations	Lm		

NEW TESTAMENT

Matthew	Mt	Ephesians	Eph	Hebrews	Heb
Mark	Mk	Philippians	Ph	James	Jm
Luke	Lk	Colossians	Col	1 Peter	1 P
John	Jn	1 Thessalonians	1 Th	2 Peter	2 P
Acts	Ac	2 Thessalonians	2 Th	1 John	1 Jn
Romans	Rm	1 Timothy	1 Tm	2 John	2 Jn
1 Corinthians	1 Cor	2 Timothy	2 Tm	3 John	3 Jn
2 Corinthians	2 Cor	Titus	Tt	Jude	Jude
Galatians	Gal	Philemon	Phm	Revelation	Rv

THE ORDINARY PATH TO HOLINESS

CHAPTER ONE

OUR CALL TO HOLINESS

Introduction

At this moment you have natural life. You did not choose to live; this life was a gift to you. The moment will come when you must die: this also is not subject to your choice. Between these two boundaries, now and the moment of death, is a lifetime of choices and responses which are of ultimate importance and significance to each person. We did not choose *to* live but we must choose *how* we will live. We do not choose to die but we must choose how we will live the years or hours or moments of our dying.

The manner of our dying is of very great importance! That moment will be considered in more detail later in this book. "Precious in the sight of the Lord is the death of His saints" (Ps 116:15). The way we choose to live and the way we choose to die are real and personal choices that constitute our response to His great gift to us of our being, our life. A way to phrase the right response to life is this: we are called to holiness. Within human life is an imperative, that we are to order our lives to the One who made us. This is simple justice, a return of what is due.

1

Living and Dying for Joy

The purpose of this book is directed to our great and human challenge, to present back to God a life worthy of His creation. He wants to help us live, and to know His life even in death, and live again. Why do I presume to write on such a lofty subject? What credentials or authority do I have for this? My credentials are weak, my authority is nonexistent; I have only an urgent imperative to share, or pass on, what I have received. I might be able to help you the reader, if you persevere, to see more clearly the ever-present One who is able to lead you into His mysterious presence. If you see how close He is even now, you will be helped. If you begin to understand the way He calls us back into Himself, the way He has always done this, you will be better able to cooperate with Him. If you see that His power to help is present and active and waiting to be received now in this moment and in all the great moments of life, then you will be helped. And I will have a small and beautiful part in your joy.

Yes, our vocation is to joy. We are called to return to our God who made us, and our return is a turn to joy. Joy is no shallow thing; it is not a superficial pleasant feeling. Joy is consistent with great suffering, and with long times of darkness and confusion. Our joy is deeply linked with our supernatural destiny, that is to say, in communion of love, in the eternal joy of God who is love.

We are made by God, and according to His purpose and intention. As we grow to understand more and more deeply the scriptural truth that God is love, or better, as we grow to *know* that love, then we see with increasing clarity that all the events of our lives are consistent with His unbounded love. Essential to our insight into this ground of truth is faith in the resurrection of Jesus Christ. It is futile to try to conclude that God is good, and loving, and just, if our view stops at the grave. We have seen too much injustice, too much cruelty, too much evil prospering in this world! Even a single isolated act of evil, escaping the human attempts at justice in this world, is enough to disprove the existence of God, if there is nothing beyond what we call death!

Human persons crave justice; in the center of our being there is a demand for truth. Seeking justice and truth, in fact we are seeking God. We experience, and if we are fortunate we realize that we experience, profound need for God in a world of separation from Him. These needs are meant to lead us to God. We need faith in God beyond us, and hope in God beyond us, with also a sharing in His love, or else our life itself is fundamentally absurd. After we are given these great supernatural graces of faith, and hope, and love, life is still not easy. With them, however, authentically human life becomes possible, full of meaning, and with joy.

The Mystery of the Cross

It is my hope that this book be for you, fellow pilgrim, a help on your journey which will not be easy but which can be beautiful. Your particular and personal path includes an invitation into the love of God in Christ Jesus, that is also an invitation into your part in His cross. Your living and your dying can comprise one integral and complete response to the one great mystery of Life. Our paths are not the same, but all paths include the possibility of radical love, perfect love. We are each given the possibility in our lives of a participation in the life of Christ Jesus, and in the love of God toward all mankind. That is to say, we all and each have an opportunity to share in His passion and cross with our cross, and to share also beyond the cross in the resurrection to eternal life.

Christ our Life; Christ our Vocation

It should be less of a puzzle than it seems to be! The means are determined by the end: when we understand the final end, we will understand the wisdom of the right means. In the mystery of creation, we who are "made in the image of God" are called to His Life. Now, because of sin, we are recalled to it as an entire race, and we must personally be reborn into it. Reborn into it, we do not instantly have the *perfection* of it, not even in a qualified and human sense of the word. A human infant has in potential the fullness of human life, but he has not attained the completeness of it. A human person who has been born "from above," reborn into the Life of Christ, does not yet have the completeness of that life, except in potential.

Completeness, maturity, perfection — these are to be achieved in time by growth. Completeness is intended in every infant; perfection is intended in every newly reborn child of God. This perfection of human life in Christ is our vocation; this is our destiny. We are called to the Life of God; we are made for a life of holiness.

Christ our Perfection

Perfection means without fault or flaw, but in a spiritual and living way. Human perfection is not to be understood in analogy with the perfection of a computer calculation, or even to the attainment of demands we unrealistically might put upon ourselves. Human perfection, rather, is the attainment of the intention that God has for us. Our Creator has shown us the standard of the perfection to which we are in fact called. Jesus Christ revealed the call: "You must be perfect, as your heavenly Father is perfect" (Mt 5:48). Jesus Christ lived the call, not as a sterile and inanimate or mathematical thing, but as a fully loving person. The Life of Jesus Christ reveals the perfection of human life and love. The imitation of His Life is a life of holiness.

God has set within every man and woman a desire for truth, for justice, and for wholehearted love. We cannot be happy except in a life of genuine virtue, a life reflecting God Himself, in whose image we are made. There are mistaken beliefs to the contrary, concerning our fundamental desires and needs, and concerning the fundamental essence of humanity itself. It is true that we human persons also hold self-centered desires for pleasure and gratification, desires which war with our deeper hunger for virtue. These baser desires confuse us; they are the fruit of confusion, and they are never satisfied. The holy image of God remains our truest and most defining mark; yet the effects of sin cannot be ignored. We are wounded deeply by the sin which surrounds us and infects our very humanity, but it has not overcome the intention of our Creator. It has not overcome the desire we have been given to know Him, to love Him, and to live with Him forever. For this reason the Gospel of Jesus Christ is good news for us; His redemption fills us with hope for the divine relationship to which we are ordered. A life of holiness is a life in response to the Gospel, the good news.

It is not the will of God that any man or woman should remain bound to a "pre-Christian world," to a world unredeemed and unenlightened by His presence. This world is perishing, it must perish, and it is good that it will, suffering as it does in deep inner contradiction. It is shot through with violence and internal strife, because it is the household of fallen Adam, and it reflects his sin. All humanity is born first into this world, and inherits the internal and external struggles of the house of Adam. Humanity is born "in Adam," in his stance of independence, and in a self-defeating inclination to what is false.

A life of holiness is a journey out of and away from the death of the house of Adam.

We are called to a new creation. We are called into a different kind of existence altogether, even in the midst of this present world. We are called into a reality that is more "real" because it is authentically human. In communion with the supernatural, it is most natural. This new reality is internally consistent with the very ground and basis of its creation. This new reality is at peace with its Creator, and it brings peace with self and neighbor. It is the kingdom of God, and of His Christ (1 Cor 15:45-49). A life of holiness is a life in His kingdom.

The Ordinary Way to the Holy Life

The new creation is entered analogously to the old: by birth. "You must be born anew" (Jn 3:7). Most of us have heard all this before, but there is a crucially important body of knowledge concerning this new creation, and new way of living, of which most of us are largely ignorant. The body of knowledge exists in the traditional Catholic theology of spiritual growth. This book presents the traditional journey to holiness, from and for the perspective of an ordinary layman. It is then a journey in ordinary holiness.

This work could be helpful for any person, but is intended especially for ordinary people, men and women, who have a growing desire to be faithful to God. I am a Catholic Christian, and married, writing then within that spirituality and state of life. I have been Protestant, and single, and I can say that this work can be helpful also to Christians within that spirituality and state. May God so bless this hope of mine! My dear Protestant brothers and sisters reading this book will have some difficulties, which I pray will be for them an incentive to understand the Catholic perspective. I know that eventually, the power of the Truth will re-gather His Church: may it be soon.

Misconceptions about the spiritual life are common. To listen to many sermons and teachings about the Christian way of life, one would think that at best the journey is an endless series of incremental improvements: millimeter by millimeter, we strive by God's grace to live more and more like Christ. Some saints miraculously achieve great sanctity, but the majority of us find ourselves content with compromise and mediocrity, a life far short of the radical Gospel call, and a long time of purgation in purgatory. We read that hard word of Jesus, "You are to be perfect, as your heavenly Father is perfect," but we quickly discount it as impossible. There is some truth in this incremental view, but it is incomplete.

Other sermons and teachings suggest that the journey is always awaiting one great leap into a New Testament reality, if we would only make that quantum leap by faith. "You must be born again," is insisted and demanded from many pulpits. If we fail to walk in the signs and miracles and fervor of which we read in Scripture, it must be our own fault, our faithlessness, our wrong thinking. This teaching generates much guilt, little if any sanctity, and sometimes even pretense of a real spirituality that is hoped for but not possessed. This quantum view also contains some truth, but is also incomplete.

The two errors described above are obviously wrong when applied to physical or emotional growth and development. Normal spiritual growth is not a simple linear progression in the soul. Who would think that an infant should grow smoothly and incrementally in thirty years to become, say, an "infant" thirty years of age and six feet in height? Everyone knows that there are definable stages of normal human growth, which differ in sharp ways from one another. A child is not merely a seven year old infant: a child is different from an infant. An adolescent is not a thirteen year old infant, nor is he merely a child six years older than he was at seven. An adolescent is not a child, and neither is he an adult. These stages have characteristics which cannot be explained as a linear addition of years. Infant, child, adolescent, adult are qualitatively different stages of life, that bring radical changes to the growing human person experiencing them. Radical newness appears and is experienced in each new stage of life. A child cannot even anticipate life as an adolescent; he is incapable of imagining accurately himself in the development he has not yet achieved. The adolescent, and then the adult, will be *himself,* the same *person*, yet also a *new self* even he cannot imagine.

Normal spiritual growth is not an instantaneous quantum change from sinner to saint. This second error is also plainly wrong when applied to physical or emotional growth and development. Who would think that adult behavior can reasonably be demanded of children? A teacher was once heard to shout at her class of loud and kinetic first-graders who were ignoring her and were completely involved in play, "Stop all this immediately and act your age!" But they were exactly acting their age: it was she who was failing to work with them in their stage of human growth. A similar failure is heard in shouts from the pulpit to just do it: just live like the great heroes of the Church. Don't we all have the same Spirit? Then what is the difference? There is a great difference between a child and an adult, and we don't reasonably expect adult behavior from children. Why then should we expect that Christian life should be instantly mature, and instantly fully developed?

Stages of Growth in Holiness

Life in the new creation is experienced gradually, but not linearly. It grows in stages, as does physical and emotional life in normal human development. In the old creation, in Adam, we proceed along our developing rational life in distinct stages: consciousness and human life grows from childhood, to adolescence, to adulthood. So in the new creation also, it is only gradually that we approach the fullness to which we are called, yet there are characteristic stages of spiritual development. Our cooperation with God our Father is greatly helped when we realize that He calls us, and is helping us, toward the fullness and maturity of life in His Son. We are called to holiness! Christ Himself is our model and our example! Yet God does not demand maturity of a child. He works with us in our childishness — gray-haired though we may be! — always working to form us into the life of His plan. The spiritual man or woman is the mature development of a spiritual "adolescent," who was once a spiritual "child" who cooperated with the grace God gives for growth and advancement toward Him.

Many Christians, sadly, do not seem to realize either the stages toward the end, or the end itself to which we are called. The Church fathers of Vatican II proclaimed clearly and beautifully the simple will of God for our holiness. "The Lord Jesus, divine teacher and model of all perfection, preached holiness of life (of which he is the author and maker) to each and every one of his disciples without distinction: 'You, therefore, must be perfect, as your heavenly Father is perfect' (Mt 5:48)."

All Christians are called to this perfection: "They must therefore hold on to and perfect in their lives that sanctification which they have received from God. They are told by the apostle to live 'as is fitting among saints' (Eph 5:3), and to put on 'as God's chosen ones, holy and beloved, compassion, kindness, lowliness, meekness, and patience' (Col 3:12), to have the fruits of the Spirit for their sanctification (cf. Gal 5:22; Rm 6:22)." Reiterating and clarifying the point, the Vatican II fathers assert, "It is therefore quite clear that all Christians in any state or walk of life are called to the fullness of Christian life and to the perfection of love."[1]

The vocation to holiness could not have been asserted by the Church more plainly. All of us are called to the same end, including the pope, the holy saints of the Church, the bishops, the nuns and religious brothers, the parish priests, the church janitor, the choir director, the busy layperson, husbands and wives, and the business executive praying in the pew. We will all stand before God for judgment; we are all called into the holiness of Christ; we are all invited into the communion of Trinitarian life; we are all judged by the standard of God's intention: "the *fullness* of Christian life" and "the *perfection of love*" (italics added). What great encouragement and consolation to know that the abundant grace of God in Christ is completely sufficient for this exalted call and expectation! Certainly the apostle Paul is able to write, "I am sure that He who began a good work in you will bring it to completion" (Ph 1:6).

An Unintended Secret: Traditional Catholic Wisdom

This book presents the traditional Catholic path toward our human destiny of spiritual maturity, in divine communion. God made us for fellowship, for a share in His perfect communion of Trinitarian love. Specifically, we need to realize that our translation from this world of confusion to a supernatural communion in God does not happen in an instant. The formation into Christ, which He is working in us through His Spirit and with His Church, has recognizable stages. Possibly Jesus was alluding to the three (now traditional) stages of spiritual growth in one of His parables of the kingdom.

> And He said, "The kingdom of God is like a man who scatters seed upon the ground, and sleeps and rises by night and day, and the seed sprouts and grows while he is unaware.

> "The earth bears fruit on its own; first the shoot, then the head of grain, and then the full grain in the head. When it is ripe, he at once sends for the sickle, because the harvest has come."   Mk 4:26-29

No farmer expects the fruit to appear in the instant the seed hits the ground! Time is needed, and is allowed. He does not expect his fruit when "the shoot" first appears, nor when he first sees "the head." He waits through the natural stages of development. The farmer tends his work; it is his investment. He cares for it, and sacrifices for it, and oversees it through the seasons until the harvest is finally ready. The three stages of growth in this parable can well suggest the three stages of growth of kingdom life in each Christian person, as has been noticed and acknowledged in traditional Catholic spiritual theology.

As the eminently reasonable St. Thomas Aquinas observed, one could say that three stages should be expected in any movement. One begins, one proceeds, and finally one arrives at the destination. To say that the spiritual life has three stages, a beginning, an intermediate stage, and a final stage is not then surprising, but this observation is not a trivial or inconsequential one. The three stages have intrinsic and important characteristics, and differ from one another in significant ways. These stages of spiritual development are stages of charity, as St. Thomas writes, and therefore are a developing participation in the supernatural love of God. That is, our essential vocation, which is a call to holiness, is realized through growth in stages. The perfection of love, which is God's intention for us and which is our destiny, should be as ordinary among us as is adulthood.

Childhood, adolescence, and adulthood have their spiritual analogies. A major difference exists, however, between physical and spiritual development. Spiritual development requires our cooperation. A person can progress toward physical adulthood merely by continuing to breathe, but more is required of emotional development and maturity, and much *much* more is required of full human spiritual development. To arrive at our call, we must cooperate with God's grace, with wisdom. The journey is greatly helped, however, if we know what to expect, and how to cooperate, and where to seek the grace of God. These are helps I hope to describe in this book: what to expect, and how to cooperate, and where to seek the necessary grace of God.

Conclusion to the Chapter

It is common for a person, upon hearing of grades of spiritual development, to right away seek to judge himself and determine "where" he is in the spiritual life. Later in the book I will present the opinion of some that *most* of us are in the beginning stages of spiritual life, either because we have never progressed further, or because we have indeed experienced something beyond, but then fell back because of fear or other reasons. Some writers will say that many have tasted the intermediate stages of spiritual life but have fallen back.

This experiencing of something beyond, which may prove too much for some, is akin physically to the crisis of adolescence. We know, in our life as human persons in this world, of the traumatic life crisis of the teen years. We joke about it, we remember our personal difficulties, we sincerely mourn the tragic choices sometimes made by friends and children of friends, in the blind passions of adolescence.

To take the risk of oversimplifying, we could say that just as the family relationships undergo change and rightly so, as a child enters adolescence, so also for a soul spiritually developing into the intermediate or adolescent stage: the spiritual family relationships must change. This analogy may be important to you personally. The crises of spiritual adolescence are powerful motivations within the soul, moving the person to a new sense of urgency. We need to understand these changes if they are occurring in us! Such persons especially need trustworthy guidance concerning religious matters! Such persons want to order their lives rightly, with a renewed sense of the brevity of life and the impending judgment upon all our lives. Such persons can then be moved to read books on spirituality and the religious life, even one like this one, as they seek the truth of God. For my part, I will try to help you, the reader, understand the spiritual development of the soul, even of *your* soul, and ways of cooperating with God along the path to holiness to which He is calling you.

As Catholics we have a rich tradition from which to learn; we have a family with many saints as brothers and sisters. We have a liturgy of worship formed according to the mind of Christ, and in concert with an eternal worship in heaven. We have an understanding of spiritual growth which is grounded in Scripture, which follows the pattern set by Jesus, and which has been taught and understood by many profoundly spiritual men and women spanning a history of many centuries. We have the sacraments, which are genuine encounters with Christ, and we have the holy Word of God. In this time of our history, we also have some great deficiencies: many of our adult Catholics have little or no personal grasp of these great treasures of the Faith, and have no time to seek them. Many do not know that they do not know, and are failing to seize this time to learn.

Lack of knowledge within the Church has profound and serious consequences. There are personal consequences: life itself becomes much more difficult and painful, stumbling from experience to experience, in darkness so to speak. After this life, much purgation awaits a soul who has not grown rightly in necessary holiness. Then there are consequences for the whole Body of Christ, weakened by ignorance, incapable of building up one another, and unable to complete the task of witness that Christ gave us. The whole rest of the world then suffers in continued confusion and darkness, not having the clear and faithful testimony of sent disciples of Christ.

The Father has always chosen and especially blessed some, that they might then be a blessing for others. This pattern finds its perfection in Christ, sent not to be served but to serve. Citing the eminent Catholic theologian Hans Urs von Balthasar, Cardinal Ratzinger quotes in his book, largely addressed to this mystery[2]: "To choose one person always means not choosing another. Yet at the same time, this chosen one, Christ, has been chosen for the sake of those not chosen...."

Cardinal Ratzinger summarizes the thesis, saying "Election is always, at bottom, election for others."[3] He surveys Scripture to find the ways of God consistent in this pattern. Hence God blessed Abel but not Cain (Gn 4), but not so that He could reject a human person He had just created even in His own image! Abel was given the special blessing of God so that he might choose to share that grace with his brother. Cain was not blessed in order that he might need to share with his brother and thus find God's favor. In this way, in God's way, both Cain and Abel could learn mutual dependence, and might enter real love for one another. In this way brotherhood is perfected. This is always God's way.

In this way God chose the descendants of Abram, so that "in you all the families of the earth shall be blessed" (Gn 12:3). Abram's family would become the chosen people, the Jews, who were to be "a light to the nations" (Is 42:6). In this way also Christ chose the first apostles: they were to carry His salvation to all the nations (Mt 28:19). In this way He chose you, and me: that we might become a blessing for others in His Name.

Let us pray for all who are called to holiness in Christ. For ourselves, may God give us the grace to grow in holiness, to grow in the living of His truth, to grow in the dying of His cross, to grow in Christian self-giving to our brothers and sisters. May Christ use us to help build and rebuild His Church.

Notes

[1] Vatican II documents, *Lumen Gentium,* 40. All quotations from the documents of Vatican II are from Austin Flannery, O.P., under the title *Vatican Council II: The Conciliar and Post-Conciliar Documents*, vol. 1 (Northport, NY: Costello Publishing, 1996).

[2] Joseph Cardinal Ratzinger, *The Meaning of Christian Brotherhood* (San Francisco: Ignatius Press, 1966), 77.

[3] Ibid., 79.

Chapter Two

GROWTH IN HOLINESS: THREE STAGES

The Traditional Stages of Spiritual Growth

The Traditional Catholic Spirituality

Catholic spirituality is not "a spirituality" which is only "for Catholics." It is universal ("catholic") in scope; it is truly human in subject, having God as object. It has a weight which deserves respect and a hearing today from both Catholics and non-Catholics. It has developed over many centuries, through the lived experience, holiness, and wisdom of many true saints. Catholic spirituality is wisdom learned in the crucible of divine testing and purification. It is simply Christianity, revealed to His holy ones in the experience of their life-offering.

A study of Catholic spiritual theology is completely practical. It has much to say to any person, hence to you in your personal journey, in the personal response to God's call to holiness. The saints and spiritually minded people who have experienced, understood, and taught this wisdom to the Church were human persons too, as you and I are. They also had doubts and fears and temptations. Many of them were at first quite

17

worldly and self-centered, before they began to seek God in earnest. They too had to begin at the beginning; they too had to make choices and changes in their lives. They too had to persevere through dark and difficult nights. They were human persons, as we are, who responded to the call and the grace of God.

Catholic spiritual theology is truly a mystical subject: it is concerned with the ultimate mystery of the Being who is absolute and yet also personal, three and also one, eternal and spirit yet also present to us who have been created in time and in matter. It is indeed the study of the relationship between God and human persons. Catholic spirituality is certainly not merely the poetic imaginings of introspective dreamers! Matters of the spirit are real; development of the human soul is as real and substantive a subject as development of the human body. The study of the development of the human soul has the additional importance, that this is a matter of eternal significance. God is Spirit. It is in that dimension, so to speak, that our relationship with Him takes place. Spiritual theology, then is a matter of ultimate importance that deals with things both crucial (our own personal lives and futures) and absolute (our relationship with God Who is Absolute Being).

It is good also to realize that Catholic spiritual theology has a consistent and continuous thread that can be traced back to Christ, if not to the beginnings of salvation history itself. That is, Catholics are not at the mercy of self-appointed guides and teachers, self-elevated to the place of expert. There are some today within our Church who seek insights and guidance in matters of the soul outside of the Catholic tradition, perhaps because they do not have the wisdom so close to them. Some then teach these spiritualities to other Catholics as though the "new" ways were somehow preferable or better than the ways of our tradition. Sometimes with a misguided sense of ecumenism, "New Age" philosophies, redecorated with Christian language, are taught in place of the spiritualities of our saints. Even some consecrated religious in our Church are chasing after the insights of Eastern gurus and seers, and ignoring the trustworthy and authentic mystics of the Catholic tradition. It is a troubling fact of our times that so many are overlooking the treasures of the Faith, while stumbling after the partial and confused insights of other religions. May God help us to keep our eyes on His truth!

Catholic spiritual theology has a long and grace-filled history. It was greatly deepened by the Carmelite doctors of the sixteenth century, and it is grounded in the rock-solid theology of St. Thomas Aquinas. This grounding in thomistic theology clarifies the point that spirituality, even what has been called "mystical" theology, is well founded in our most respected, objective and conservative theological framework. Spiritual or mystical theology, when experienced, is an intensely personal reality, but it must not be thought of as merely subjective. The work of God in the human soul, to purify the person and draw him into the communion of the Holy Trinity, is objective and real.

Our concern, in other words, is not only with individual experience as such, but with objectively real personal human growth toward God. Humanity has fallen; God is redeeming human persons. Our understanding is not any attempt for the latest and the newest, but that which has been proven over time in the lives of saints. The model of spiritual growth in three stages has been accepted as trustworthy in the Catholic Church for centuries.

St. Thomas helps us, seeing with his characteristic clarity the essential simplicity of the heart of spiritual theology: God is working charity in us. Charity is the crucial, necessary substance of our spiritual life.[1] Persons immersed in Western culture today have difficulty not only living a life of charity, but even in understanding the concept. Charity is simply love for God, and love for others because of God. It is this conscious presence of God at the beginning and at the end of charity, that clarifies its distinction from love. Right understanding of charity enables us to see how it is possible to love neighbors we hardly know, enemies we would rather not know, and sometimes friends we know too well. To share in God's love, to have this virtue of charity, we experience love for these persons not primarily for who they are but because of God. We love them because of who God is; first we love God in them, and them in God.

Thomas sees, then, the traditional "three ways" of the human journey as a progression of the soul in stages into divine charity. The three ways of spiritual theology is acknowledged by traditional doctors of the Church ranging from Thomas Aquinas and Augustine to those more typically thought of as "mystical" — John of the Cross, and Catherine of Siena, and others as well.

Two classical works on Catholic spiritual theology have been recently republished, and offer Christians today very helpful references for study. Fr. Reginald Garrigou-Lagrange and Fr. John Arintero, both Dominicans, have provided excellent surveys of traditional Catholic spirituality to the Church. Both include copious quotes from the fathers, doctors, and saints who have contributed so beautifully to our collective wisdom. Fr. Garrigou-Lagrange[2] offers perhaps a more systematic perspective, and writes with both clarity and unction. A great strength of Fr. Arintero's work,[3] following the early fathers of the Church, is his vision of divine adoption that carries us into the very family of God, and hence into divinity itself (by participation, of course, and not by nature). A third contemporary work, by Fr. Jordan Aumann,[4] is also excellent. Fr. Aumann takes as his framework of the journey not the traditional three ways, but the grades of prayer (following mostly St. Teresa of Avila) which the soul experiences along the way. Fr. Garrigou-Lagrange's work includes and synthesizes both perspectives (both Teresa's framework of prayer, through her "mansions" in the soul, and the traditional "three ways").

Much misunderstanding exists today regarding the mystical life. Some, even among those who are highly educated in theology, have received only the briefest, inadequate education in the science of spiritual development. Some who have received good formal teaching in the subject have not really profited from it because of their own lack of personal spiritual growth. These are unable to understand the information they have received because of a lack of the corresponding spiritual experience and wisdom. The lack of understanding in many teachers within the Church has resulted in an even more widespread lack of understanding among ordinary lay men and women. Misunderstandings and ignorance have then been passed on, sowing confusion and leading to the wasting of much grace.

Fr. Garrigou-Lagrange finds that the great Catholic advances in Christian spirituality have been today mostly ignored. In our contemporary situation, even some "experts" confuse the full normal development of the life of grace on earth with what is only the very beginning of it.[5] That is, spiritual childhood has been interpreted as spiritual adulthood. Some souls who are seeking spiritual guidance, amid this contemporary ignorance, have been led to believe that they have reached the highest and final of the stages of spiritual development when, in fact, they are only beginning the journey. This is a major error, with consequences. The result of the misguidance and misdirection is grievous for the spiritual growth of the individual and of the Church, because real actual perfection is our goal. Fr. Garrigou-

Lagrange finds that the traditional and scriptural standard of perfection has in effect been lowered, and souls are deprived of the real goal of spiritual maturity that God has made us to long for and to grow toward. That true end of personal full and mature relationship with God, which is a true hope, is a great stimulant to a life of generosity and fervor, and zeal for close and obedient union with Him.[6] Mediocre goals in the spiritual life cannot but quench the zeal of the Spirit, and cannot but tend to a lukewarm Church which is hardly adequate to the evangelical call and will of Christ.

A second error prevalent today is the belief that there are two different paths which God desires for His people: a harder path for the great and the heroic, for the blessed saints, but an easier path for ordinary Christians. The Church teaches plainly, however, that there is one call for every man and woman: all are called to holiness. Nor are there two ways to union with God — one ordinary and the other extraordinary to which most of us could never aspire — but rather there is one way. There is not one Christianity for common people, and another for visionaries and mystics, and perhaps a third for severe ascetics. There is one path, one journey or way which leads from death in sin, to holiness with God in the beatific vision.

It is true that there is great variety in the ways of God with men and women, Who as a loving Father deals with each of us as individuals and persons. Yet it is also true to say that there is one way for all of fallen humanity. Christ focuses us on the single path: "I am the way, and the truth, and the life; no one comes to the Father except through Me" (Jn 14:6). Despite the variations in perspective (by writers with such varied styles as John of the Cross, Bonaventure, and Teresa of Avila for example), and the existentially personal nature of the real divine encounter, we should not lose sight of the singleness and unity of the way. There are many personal journeys; there is one way: Christ.

Fr. Garrigou-Lagrange has presented a comprehensive overview of Catholic spiritual tradition from the patristic era, through the Latin and Greek fathers, to the medieval theologians.[7] He has surveyed the spiritual works of the saints, a great source for guidance in the journey.[8] Although he finds variation in the detail of the pictures presented among them, he is able to organize and synthesize a consistent Catholic view using the framework of the three ways. One of the great treasures of the Church (largely unknown and unused today) is this highly developed understanding within spiritual or mystical theology, which explains and describes the ministry of the Word in the formation and development of the soul.

St. John of the Cross speaks for many, among spiritual writers, of the need for good and precise teaching on the spiritual journey, for "it is extremely necessary to so many souls." He acknowledges that many may fail to complete the goal, falling short of their potential. "Occasionally, it is the desire which is lacking, or they are not willing to let themselves be led therein. At times, it is because of ignorance, or because they vainly seek an experienced guide capable of leading them to the summit."[9] The traditional way for earnest Catholic souls seeking holiness has been to seek a trustworthy spiritual director and confessor, who could help as a "soul-friend" along the admittedly hard road of Christian life.

Catholics do not lack sources of wisdom and direction along the path; ours is a Church of many treasures. Ordinary priests of extraordinary sanctity can be found in the Church, serving their brothers and sisters with priestly service, counsel and the rich example of their lives. Our tradition has a wealth of writers and saints, including John of the Cross, Teresa of

Avila, Thérèse of Lisieux, Catherine of Siena, and many others. The sacraments of the Church provide grace for spiritual growth, and cooperate with the interior work of the Holy Spirit in the soul. Even if a personal spiritual director cannot be found, the soul is not left entirely alone. As will be emphasized later in the book, great assistance to ordinary laypeople along their spiritual journey is provided within the Church. The Church is truly mother to us, providing for us through her ordinary means of grace in the sacraments, including the beautiful sacrament of matrimony, and especially the most holy sacrifice of the Mass.

St. Thomas and the Perfection of Charity

St. Thomas Aquinas refers to three stages in explaining the growth toward Christian perfection. In what does perfection consist? Thomas states simply: "Primarily and essentially the perfection of the Christian life consists in charity, principally as to the love of God, secondarily as to the love of our neighbor...."[10] This point is essential. In speaking of the spiritual journey, and in investigating such spiritual concepts as contemplation and union with God in prayer, we are concerned not with "mystical experience" for its own sake: we are concerned with charity, in which the Christian obedience of faith consists.

Thomas responds to the question, "Ought we to mark three stages in charity, beginning, progressing, and perfect?" The answer is yes. He finds that distinction can be made and differences observed among the three stages corresponding to one's growth in charity, as one moves away from a life of sin, toward a participation in the love of God. He describes the stages very briefly.

1. *The Beginning Stage.* Beginning the Christian life, the believer finds that most of his concern and effort is made withdrawing from sin and resisting the appetites which drive him away from charity. Beginners need to nourish and carefully foster charity to prevent its loss, and they need to avoid falling back to the ways they have just left. Attacks of temptation disturb the peace of the soul in this stage, but after struggle and perseverance, the believer can give his mind to making progress.

2. *The Progressing Stage.* In this second stage, a certain measure of victory over temptation has been achieved. Most of the effort of the soul is now directed to advancing in virtue, with the concern that charity grow and become strong. This is the stage of those who are making progress in the journey.

3. *The Stage of the Perfect.* In this third stage, which is not static but which also involves progress, most effort is made cleaving to God, and enjoying Him. In this stage are Christians of heroic virtue, who sincerely long to leave this earth and be with Him.[11]

St. Bernard and Four Degrees of Charity

St. Thomas did not "devise" this structure of stages in a vacuum, of course. We will see that the three stages are evident even in Scripture, in the formative method of Jesus Himself. In the century just preceding St. Thomas (d. 1274), St. Bernard of Clairvaux (d. 1153) contributed his part in the Church's understanding of these developmental stages of charity.[12] St. Bernard described four degrees because he began with that degree of charity in a person before conversion itself; for St. Thomas, the first degree of true charity is that possible after conversion and Baptism when charity is infused into the soul with the other virtues of faith and hope.

St. Bernard's first degree of charity is that found in a person before conversion, when he loves himself in a selfish way, and others as they benefit him. God, love for God, and love for others because of God are not realities even on the horizon of this person. This person might use the word "love" in reference to other persons or to things, but his meaning is always centered upon himself and the good that these persons or things do for him. In our present usage of the word *charity*, then, as love for God and for others because of God, this person does not possess charity. This stage in the life of a person is an important one to understand, however, because it is a common one and the starting point for all in original sin. The self-centered perspective of this "degree of charity" remains a temptation and a danger for all even after Baptism. How easy it can be to view things and even other persons as means for my good, my pleasure, my ends! This, then, is St. Bernard's first degree of charity.

St. Bernard's second degree of charity occurs when the person discovers God, and sees that God is essential to his good. The degree of charity now awakened in the person coincides with that first degree of St. Thomas, brought on by the experience of repentance and initial conversion. He begins to love God, although not for Who God is, but rather for what God can do for him. He perceives that he cannot exist by himself but only by the will of God, and that his future is dependent upon God. He "begins then by faith to seek after God, and to love Him as something necessary to his own welfare. That is the second degree, to love God, not for God's sake, but selfishly."[13] This is the second degree of charity according to St. Bernard, which corresponds to the first degree of St. Thomas.

The third degree of charity according to St. Bernard begins after the person discovers, in his seeking after the things of God, the great and divine beauty of God in Himself. Bernard writes,

> But when, in truth, on account of his own necessity he has begun to worship and come to Him again and again by meditating, by reading, by prayer and by being obedient, little by little God becomes known to him through experience, in a sort of familiarity; and consequently He grows more lovable, and thus by tasting how sweet the Lord is (cf. Ps 34:9), he passes to the third degree so that he loves God now, not for his own sake but for Himself.[14]

This purer and more sublime degree of charity corresponds to that described in St. Thomas's second degree, the progressing stage. This depth of charity is still not pure or complete, but is limited by the self-love and self-centeredness that remain in the person. Traces of mercenary motivations still affect and infect, so to speak, the acts of the person.

In the final stage of this progression, the most pure charity is developed. In the fourth degree of St. Bernard, God becomes all in all. The person loves God above all else, and loves all in God. Even oneself, one's own life and person, is loved only in God. Here the heroic virtue even unto martyrdom is revealed. Bernard very humbly writes of the third degree, prior to the heights of this fourth degree of charity,

> Surely he must remain long in this state; and I know not whether it would be possible to make further progress in this life to that fourth degree and perfect condition wherein man loves himself solely for God's

sake. Let any who have attained so far bear record; I
confess it seems beyond my powers.[15]

This fourth degree corresponds to that described as the third
degree of St. Thomas, the stage of the perfect.

The Three Stages in Scripture

The pattern of the three stages is reflected in the New Testament, in the journey of discipleship which was actually experienced by the apostles. This evidence for the three stages is
highly significant: it places the gradations of the spiritual journey clearly in the intention of Christ, as He led His chosen ones
from ordinary lives in the world to become authentic and powerful witnesses of Christian life. That is, the Christian formation of the apostles by Christ Himself shows three distinct and
unique phases. Their encounter with God, and their interior
spiritual formation, show three successive stages of increasingly deep relationship and increasingly profound commitment.
Fr. Garrigou-Lagrange describes this pattern, which he finds
observed by several writers.[16]

The first stage of the discipleship of the apostles extends
from their conversion to follow Jesus, up to the time of His passion. In this stage we find, in the apostles, behavior characteristic of beginners in the spiritual life. This corresponds to that
called the purgative way, or the way of beginners, by Catholic
writers. The apostles had indeed made a commitment to the
Lord, having "left everything" (Lk 5:11) to follow Him, yet their
example at this point is still far from heroic. Peter exhibits
much, in this stage, that "ordinary Christians" can identify with.
The Peter of "little faith" (Mt 14:31) during the earthly ministry of Jesus was far different from the courageous apostle after

Pentecost. In the profound crisis of the passion, even Peter seemed to fall completely from his vocation. Yet this apparent failure was a dark night which was to precede a new dawn, and which would lead him to a second conversion, with a new stage of his relationship with Christ. Similar turning, and returning, occurred for the other apostles as well. The curious combination of faith with lack of faith, of struggle against the understandably human failings of common human persons: all this is typical of the beginning stage of discipleship. It is demonstrated for us in the Gospels, by the apostles, before the passion of Christ.

The second stage of the spiritual journey of the first Christians extended from the passion of Christ to the ascension. This corresponds to that called the way of proficients, or the illuminative way, by traditional Catholic writers on spirituality. In this stage the apostles were "still fearful; their faith still needed to be enlightened, their hope to be strengthened, their charity to be endowed with the necessary zeal."[17] In the forty days before the ascension, the apostles learned from Jesus in a totally new and different way, and found a new and profoundly deeper relationship with Him. This stage led to and ended with a second privation, a second trial, a second dark night which was a necessary part of their formation. The now spiritual, and yet also sensible and even tangible presence of the risen Christ among them, was not to be their final experience of Him. They had to experience His ascension and second departure from them, as a similar privation to their first loss through His death on the cross.

Between their loss of His physical presence among them, in His death on the cross, and their second loss of His resurrected presence among them in His ascension to the Father, the disciples of Jesus knew Him in a radically different way. This was a time of greatly deepened intimacy with Him, yet still they were imperfect and lacking "power from on high" (Lk 24:49). The apostles demonstrate for us here, in their discipleship between the resurrection and the ascension, that intermediate stage of spiritual formation which is now called, in traditional Catholic spirituality, the illuminative way.

The third stage began with Pentecost, a "third conversion,"[18] a new spiritual transformation which carried them into Christian fullness and maturity. This stage corresponds to that called the way of the perfect, or the unitive way, in Catholic spiritual theology. Here their souls were greatly enlightened, their wills greatly strengthened to live a Christian life of heroic virtue. As beginners they were with Christ yet in a worldly way, then they were with Him in the forty days in a new and more spiritual way, yet still not perfectly. But after Pentecost, they experienced the life to which they were called and ordered from the beginning. After Pentecost they lived heroic and sacrificial lives of virtue, even unto martyrdom. The apostles demonstrate for us in this phase of their formation the examples of Christian lives worthy of saints. Christians whom we recognize today as saints are those who have attained a life of such sanctity, a life of real *human* spiritual perfection and maturity.

The spiritual formation of the apostles is seen to be, then, in a sequence of three different phases, or stages. These stages are not merely continuously improving, incrementally deepening growths in faithfulness. The stages differ in kind more than in degree, as deep interior change takes place in the believer. The difference is more akin to that distinguishing childhood, adolescence, and adulthood, than that distinguishing say a college freshman, a sophomore, and a junior. To make a comparison more to the point, the difference from stage to stage is more essential than that which most adult Christians experience after the same calendar time as the apostles experienced with Christ: three years as a disciple, then an additional fifty days following the passion, then after another day (Pentecost). Our process of formation today seldom produces the results we see under the formation and teaching of Christ with His apostles! Yet the Church is commanded to do this, to effect such formation, whatever the time required. The apostles were commanded to go and make disciples, "teaching them to observe all that I have commanded you" (Mt 28:20).

The Parable of the Sower

The familiar parable of the sower in Matthew's Gospel takes on new possibilities of meaning in the light of the three-stage path of discipleship revealed in the Gospels by the Lord. Because Jesus demonstrated this movement of formation in transforming His followers, it takes on a normative significance. We can hear the parable of the sower in this light, and we discover in this teaching of Jesus these three stages of kingdom growth. The parable, Jesus himself explains, concerns the fruitfulness of the word of the kingdom. He, the Word, sows this word upon the hearts of hearers. Remembering that the development of this word into living and fruitful faith occurs in time and in stages, we listen again to the parable.

And He told them many things in parables, saying: "A sower went out to sow. And as he sowed, some seeds fell along the path, and the birds came and devoured them.

"Other seeds fell on rocky ground, where they had not much soil, and immediately they sprang up, since they had no depth of soil, but when the sun rose they were scorched; and since they had no root they withered away.

"Other seeds fell upon thorns, and the thorns grew up and choked them. Other seeds fell on good soil and brought forth grain, some a hundredfold, some sixty, some thirty.

"He who has ears, let him hear."   Mt 13:3-9

In the light of Pentecost we understand how cutting is that last pronouncement. The word searches the hearts of persons and divides them into two groups, two cities, two ways of living. It is sharper than any two-edged sword, and divides individuals, as well as humanity. The word demands a decision of its hearers.

The Word Divides Mankind:
Some Hear, Some Do Not Hear

Then the disciples came and said to Him, "Why do You speak to them in parables?"

And He answered them, "To you it has been given to know the secrets of the kingdom of heaven, but to them it has not been given.

"For to him who has, will more be given, and he will have abundance; but from him who has not, even what he has will be taken away.

"This is why I speak to them in parables, because seeing they do not see, and hearing they do not hear, nor do they understand.

"With them indeed is fulfilled the prophecy of Isaiah which says: 'You shall indeed hear but never understand, and you shall indeed see but never perceive. For this people's heart has grown dull, and their ears are heavy of hearing, and their eyes they have closed, lest they should perceive with their eyes, and hear with their ears, and understand with their heart, and turn for me to heal them.'

"But blessed are your eyes, for they see, and your ears, for they hear.

"Truly, I say to you, many prophets and righteous men longed to see what you see, and did not see it, and to hear what you hear, and did not hear it."

Mt 13:10-17

In this passage we must note something of the results in the lives of the two groups of persons, after their encounter with the living and dividing word of God. We quickly want to number three groups of persons in this parable, according to the three types of ground: a group for the rocky ground, a group for the thorns, and a group for the good ground. But before there are those three that show some viability, there is the group of persons pictured by the barren path. In other words, the first division taught in the parable is the division into two groups: one group does not hear, the other does hear. Those who have been granted to really hear these treasures in mystery will be promised "more," even an "abundance." We note that *growth*, stretching into and needing future time, is indicated, for they have now and will be given more. The eyes and ears of these persons, who can receive, are "blessed." It is only the blessed group that will be further grouped into three, corresponding to the three stages of kingdom development.

Those not granted to hear with understanding are left with only nonenduring possessions, and they are destined to lose all that they now hold. Is it the grasping of the transient treasures of this world that indeed makes their heart "dull" to the living word? In the crucial choice between the two masters to serve, is it a choice of Mammon, the god of this world, that closes the heart of a person to the truths of God? In the light of Pentecost we must see this tragic blindness and deafness which so hardens the heart of a human person that he will refuse the healing touch of Christ. The word divides now, as it is sown among human persons, as it will divide finally and ultimately on the Day of Judgment.

The Way of the Lost

"Hear then the parable of the sower.
"When any one hears the word of the kingdom and does not understand it, the evil one comes and snatches away what is sown in his heart; this is what was sown along the path."   Mt 13:18-19

There is great irony in this passage, that it is "along the path" that exactly no progress can be made! The "paths" of this world are illusions, to those with spiritual discernment, compared with the true journey which faces human persons. We are but pilgrims, called as Abram was (Gn 12:1 ff.), to strike off for an unknown and unseen land of great promise. Our pilgrimage is discovered, however, to be essentially an interior one. The word is sown in the heart: it is in the heart that openness to God is found, or is not found, bears fruit, or does not bear fruit.

The Way of Beginners

"As for what was sown on rocky ground, this is he who hears the word and immediately receives it with joy; yet he has no root in himself, but endures for a while, and when tribulation or persecution arises on account of the word, immediately he falls away."
Mt 13:20-21

"Tribulation" and "persecution" became a fearful and real threat for the disciples of Christ during the passion. Knowing the characteristically bold behavior of St. Peter during the earthly ministry of Jesus, but then his fear and denials during the trial and crucifixion, we can hear how well this passage describes him and in fact all the apostles. They all ran in fear, initially. The word "rocky" (*petrodes*) recalls the very name Jesus gave to Simon Peter (*Petros*). The immediate, impulsive nature of Peter in the days before the passion is well noted. The falling away "when tribulation or persecution arises on account of the word" describes painfully but accurately the fall and denials of Peter in the shadow of the cross of Christ.

All of the apostles ran away and left Him under the threat of persecution. We see then that this is a parabolic example that is very appropriate to the beginning stage of Christian formation, which the apostles themselves experienced between conversion and the passion of Christ. This initial stage of Christian formation, as has been noted, is the biblical pattern for what was later termed the stage of the beginner, or the purgative stage.

The stage is called purgative by Catholic writers because it is devoted to the purgation of the soul of obvious and sensual sins. This is the time for separating oneself from serious sin, from mortal sins, and from the obvious lusts of the world. The disciples picture this for us in leaving all they had, and following Jesus. The seven capital sins of pride, sloth, envy, anger, avarice, gluttony, and luxury are ones to which Christians are most inclined in this time of beginners, as St. Thomas points out, because these sins all spring from inordinate self-love.[19] It is this self-love which is disordered, which is antagonistic to the love of God that is life for us. This self-love must be purged from the soul in this stage. Hence we hear in these "rocks" within the heart of the beginner, just that inordinate self-love that obstructs the life of God within.

In terms of this parable, then, we see that the positive appropriate activity of the beginner in the Christian life is the removal of those rocks. This is the time of active purgation, and active work and prayer directed to the removal from one's life of these obvious sins, causes of sins, and occasions of sin which impede the life of the kingdom. Negatively, the dangers in temptation and persecution are obvious. A disciple who appears bold and courageous before the burning heat bears down upon him, had better listen soberly. A beginning disciple having a strong but inordinate sense of self, with its consequent inordinate self-love, can witness his bravado turn to vapor in the face of death.

Inordinate self-love runs from the cross, as Peter and the others did. Yet it is precisely the cross and its conflict, loss, and suffering which can be the occasion of the "second conversion" leading to the deeper and renewed Christian life of the illuminative stage of the proficients.

The Way of the Proficient

> "As for what was sown among thorns, this is he who hears the word, but worldly cares and the deception of wealth choke the word, and it proves unfruitful."
>
> Mt 13:22

If our pattern of interpretation holds, then we will hear in this passage a teaching particularly appropriate to the apostle's formation between the resurrection and Pentecost, a teaching appropriate to the stage called the illuminative way. It is true that in a first hearing of the parable, we typically interpret the three sown areas of ground as three different types of heart in three different types of persons, having three different final outcomes. The whole of Scripture, however, does not allow us to keep that interpretation.

The history of the apostles shows us that persons who fail to show fruit in "tribulation and persecution" — that is, persons who are described in the parable by the seed sown on "rocky ground" — can be given a second chance. The "rocky ground" cannot be an unchangeable and innate quality of the heart; it must admit of change and improvement. The ultimately fruitful and faithful lives of the apostles proves to us that the "rocky ground" of the parable must somehow be changeable into the "good ground" of the last part of the story. It must be possible for those hard and barren "rocks" in the heart of a human person to be cleared away. Such an experience in the heart of a person is in fact the fulfillment of a prophecy of the Old Testament, "And I will give them a new heart, and put a new spirit within them; I will take the stony heart out of their flesh and give them a heart of flesh" (Ezk 11:19, 36:26). In spite of failures in the early days, years, or even decades of Christian life, we have a right to real hope! Peter denied the Lord in the first stage of his Christian discipleship, but the story does not end there. God is greater than the hardness in our hearts: the parable continues, and the sower continues his mysterious and redemptive work.

We continue to listen, then, and wonder if the thorny ground of the parable represents the behavior of the apostles during the forty days, that is, the illuminative stage of spiritual growth in general. The Lord tells us that the thorns represent "worldly cares and the deception of wealth." We remember, certainly, the prominent place of worldly concern among the apostles in this time, even after witnessing the risen Lord. We remember also their perspective on the purpose of His coming: "Lord, will you at this time restore the kingdom to Israel?"

(Ac 1:6). Does their concern not reveal a delight still in *worldly* riches, and a kingdom still defined in earthly terms? The impossible contradiction of this earthly expectation was unmasked in the crown of *thorns* set upon the head of the King in His Hour. His kingdom is not of this world, and there is no abiding place of compromise.

The spiritual understanding of the apostles during this stage of the forty days is indeed greater than the worldly perspective of their days before the passion, and less than that of their heroic supernatural virtue which came after Pentecost. They have achieved a certain faith in the resurrection power of Christ, yet it is not perfect and it is not incorporated personally within them. The crown of thorns proclaims painfully the contrast between the kingdoms of this world, and the kingdom of God. It judges the unreal hopes for some "middle ground," some compromise position, in the life of a Christian. We can hear in these "thorns" spiritual impediments particularly appropriate to the stage of proficients. Thorns are rooted in the soul; they are growing and living alongside the divine word planted there. Thorns are a more subtle obstruction to fruitfulness than are rocks, as venial sins are than mortal sins. Thorns draw life away from the growth of the word, and in fact "choke" the growth of the word so that it cannot bear fruit. The thorns cannot bear fruit by their nature: they can only grow, and choke and entangle the life of God within, and in hidden ways. A Christian in the illuminative stage loves God, and has tasted his life. But he begins to feel the thorny pricks of conscience which reveal just how mercenary is his love, and how deeply rooted is his own concupiscence.

Because they are rooted in the soul, thorns are more subtle in their effects, and less obvious than the rocks and stones which were the main concern before. Rocks are alien and obstructive, but they are not attached or growing within the very life of the soul. Thorns require a deeper purgation, a second dark night, and what Fr. Garrigou-Lagrange calls the "third conversion." The apostles experienced this next purgation and purification within them in the ascension. The Christ they had experienced in the forty days, who demonstrated supernatural powers to them, who comforted them and gave them great joy, was then lifted up and ascended out of their sight. They had to experience the loss of Christ again, differently, at a deeper spiritual level, beyond their loss of Him physically by the cross, in order to experience the life of God within them, in a new way, at Pentecost.

The Way of the Perfect

"As for what was sown on good soil, this is he who hears the word and understands it; he indeed bears fruit, and yields, in one case a hundredfold, in another sixty, and in another thirty."   Mt 13:23

Here, in the soil of the heart now free of the rocks of the beginning stage, and now cleansed even of the deeply rooted thorns of the more advanced illuminative stage, the sown word can bring forth the fruit of God's intention. Fruit was promised to the disciples in the shadow of the cross, when Christ was still among them in the flesh. "You did not choose Me, but I chose you and appointed you that you should go and bear fruit, and that your fruit should abide; so that whatever you ask the Father in My name, He may give it to you" (Jn 15:16). Through the Spirit-filled Church after Pentecost came fulfillment of the word of Christ, "Truly, truly, I say to you, he who believes in Me will also do the works that I do; and greater works than these will he do, because I go to the Father" (Jn 14:12).

The book of Acts documents a Church of supernatural power, enabled and enlivened by the Holy Spirit of God. Here is the perfection of charity in human persons: lives ordered to the will of God, for the sake of the love of God. Here we read of lives of self-donation, of individuals presenting their bodies "a living sacrifice" (Rm 12:1), of persons truly loving their neighbors for the sake of the love of God. This is the perfection of the Christian life, the heroic perfection of the virtue of charity.

The Traditional Three Stages

The spiritual formation of the apostles by the ministry of the Word among them proceeded in time, in three distinct phases of transformation. God took them from where they were, as common persons, to uncommon lives of heroic virtue. We see in His work three stages of spiritual development which are parallel to the natural growth stages of a human person. We see far different physical characteristics in a child, an adolescent, and an adult. Radical changes occur in a child at puberty, which reach completion in adulthood. We would not send a child to the physical labor that requires the strength of a man or woman; we would even be careful of our physical expectations of an adolescent. Thus the apostles were told to wait: "And behold, I am sending the promise of My Father upon you; so stay in the city until you are clothed with power from on high" (Lk 24:49).

In emotional development also, there is clearly a development in time that occurs from childhood through adolescence to adulthood. We do not expect a child really to act as an adult, even though we hold out adult behavior as a model for him. Of an adolescent we expect more, but also with some leniency, knowing that his maturing process is not yet completed. The head of a family having members at all three stages of development, is careful to accommodate himself to them in his expectations and in his provisions for them.

The spiritual analogy is obvious. The onset of rationality, separating infancy from childhood, is analogous to conversion and acceptance of God — a most rational human act. The stages of spiritual formation then follow, from beginner to proficient to the perfect, leading to our goal: "until we all attain to the unity of faith and knowledge of the Son of God, to mature manhood, to the extent of Christ's full stature" (Eph 4:13).

We need to understand the norms and expectations appropriate to each spiritual stage. Why? Because it is good for a child to know that he is a child and to be a child: he is not an adolescent; he is not an adult. It is good for an adolescent to know that he is an adolescent and to be an adolescent: he is not a child; he is not an adult. It is good for an adult to care appropriately both for children and for adolescents, that he might help them to grow to their own full potential. God our loving Father is pleased to work within these stages, physically and spiritually. He accommodates His expectations of us and His provisions for us to that which is appropriate. We will see later how the liturgy of the Mass, for example, provides for each stage, and works within persons in each stage for the ultimate calling to perfection in Christ. For now, we will explore the characteristics of the three stages in more detail, to better understand the road set before us, the road to our final end with God in the fellowship of the Holy Trinity. Fr. Garrigou-Lagrange summarized his extensive study of the many writers in Catholic tradition, and condensed the following marks of each of the three stages.[20]

The Purgative Way

Newly incorporated into Christ, the converted and baptized are called to walk in conversion, toward God and away from sin. They are walking even as beginners toward the cross, seeking to die to sin more and more.

> Put to death therefore what is earthly in you: fornication, impurity, passion, evil desire, and covetousness, which is idolatry... put them all away: anger, wrath, malice, slander, and foul talk from your mouth. Do not lie to one another, seeing that you have put off the old nature with its practices and have put on the new nature, which is being renewed in knowledge after the image of its Creator.
>
> Col 3:5 -10

This stage of the spiritual life is a time of purgation and cleansing, of separation from the recently abandoned ways of the old man. Paul exhorts the Christians in Rome,

> We know that our old self was crucified with him so that the sinful body might be destroyed, and we might no longer be enslaved to sin. For he who has died is freed from sin. But if we have died with Christ, we believe that we shall also live with Him.... So you also must consider yourselves dead to sin and alive to God in Christ Jesus. Let not sin therefore reign in your mortal bodies, to make you obey their passions.
>
> Rm 6:6-12

A Christian in the purgative way, a beginner, must actively pursue this basic attitude of turning and returning. An older person, having habits of the old nature well established in him, must acknowledge his real need to turn and "become as a child" to enter the kingdom of heaven. Discipleship in this stage is a continuing recall to the basic and fundamental message of the Gospel, a life ordered to the Sermon on the Mount, a focus on the true end of humanity, a reminder of the futility of the world, an exhortation to all the means of grace for help in the spiritual struggle, and a building by all means available of the sanctifying grace necessary for Christian life. It is crucially important for the beginner to turn away from all sin, to turn to the Lord Jesus Christ, and to remain close to Him.

Unique to this stage is the active role of the person in God's work. It is entirely appropriate that the person be exhorted and encouraged to *do* what is right, to *choose* his way, to *go* to the means of grace, to *stop* any sin he is in. It is correspondingly appropriate that the beginner in this stage seek such counsel, and earnestly strive to live it. In short, following the scriptural pattern for this stage, the beginner must seek to follow Jesus as the first disciples followed Jesus, in a simple and childlike way, remaining with Him even as the scandal of the cross gets nearer and nearer.

The First Dark Night, and the "Second Conversion"

The transitional boundary that separates the beginning stage from the second, or illuminative stage, is crucial in the life of the soul. In the normative example of Scripture, in the formation by Christ of the apostles, this boundary was the passion and the cross of Christ. The personal experience in the soul of this transition to a profoundly deeper relationship with the Lord is called the "second conversion." It is a particularly important event for several reasons. First, it is a confusing, even bewildering experience to the soul, over which the person has no control. A crisis of some sort has crept in or crashed upon the person, leaving his whole perspective shaken or lost. Former ways of dealing with life are no longer appropriate; former methods of prayer no longer give consolation; one's former relationship with God Himself is no longer the same. It is not possible here to give complete discussion of this event, but suffice it to say that the soul is tempted to draw back from further progress. For those who continue, the way of illumination has begun, and experiences of infused contemplation bring a totally new relationship with God, and totally new demands upon his Christian response.

Many, however, do not continue through this trying crisis. One spiritual writer, in a short but full synthesis of the work of John of the Cross and Teresa of Avila, asserted that *most* people never advance out of the beginning stage. "This is the stage at which the majority of Christians remain all their lives, sad to say, so that purgatory has to accomplish what they left undone on earth."[21]

Fr. Benedict Groeschel analyzes this phenomenon of shrinking back from spiritual growth through the dark night from a psychological as well as a spiritual perspective. He writes that the possibilities facing the soul toward the end of the dark night of trial are too bright, too exalted: the person actually fears the possibility of real happiness and fulfillment. Other persons perhaps begin to go on, advancing in spirituality, but wrongly believing that the trials are now over for good. When trials reappear in new and different ways, the soul is confused and retreats.

Another fear Groeschel suggests is instructive: the fear of a life without self-seeking. The dark night of trial brings the new perspective that I am not the center of the universe! Deeper insights which follow illumine more and more clearly the imperfections and flaws of the soul. Groeschel notes, "Spiritual writers have pointed out that the relative freedom of the illuminative way is often more frightening because one may become aware of more deeply rooted conflicts."[22] The illuminative way demands even more of the Christian, not less, as perhaps many souls mistakenly wish.

Writing of this crucial transition, St. Teresa of Avila notes that many souls do indeed enter it. Her formulation of the spiritual life is not in the three stages as such, but in a picture of seven mansions within the soul. The numbered mansions are progressively closer to full union with God. There is not complete agreement on exactly how to align the seven mansions with the three stages of the soul. Some other writers place Teresa's mansions one and two in the purgative stage, mansions three and four in the illuminative stage, and mansions five through seven in the unitive stage. For several reasons, however, this book will hold to the following correspondence: Teresa's mansions one, two and three are in the purgative stage; mansions four and five are in the illuminative stage; mansions six and seven are in the unitive stage.

Teresa writes of the fourth mansions, which would correspond to the illuminative stage: "It is," she says, " the one which the greatest number of souls enter."[23] Speaking of its critical and spiritually dangerous character: "As the natural is united with the supernatural in it, it is here that the Devil can do most harm." She explains that in higher mansions, the Lord gives him fewer opportunities.[24] In this stage, the possibilities are crucial — to persevere and advance, or to fall back.

The Illuminative Way

Transition within the soul to this stage of relationship with God is revealed through changes in prayer and by the experience of the "second conversion." Remembering that this stage is parallel to the original formation of the apostles in their experiences between the passion and Pentecost, we realize that the Christian here begins to truly accept the cross in his life, and experiences in his soul the reality of the resurrection. Christ has indeed conquered death! He is in fact, and *personally*, both "my Lord and my God" (Jn 20:28).

Paul writes that the Christian, in the light of faith and under the inspiration of the Holy Spirit which has been breathed into the Church, has "put on the new nature, which is being renewed in knowledge after the image of its creator." Hence, "put on then, as God's chosen ones, holy and beloved, compassion, kindness, lowliness, meekness and patience... and above all these put on love, which binds everything together in perfect harmony" (Col 3:10-14). Persons in this stage are called to a deeper following of Christ, an interior conformity to Him. We are called to imitate Him and those who are like Him, the saints. We must have His sentiments, His passion, His self-donation, His love.

Besides the deeper interior nature of this stage of conversion is the uniquely passive nature of it, contrasted with the active purgation of the beginning stage. This work is the work of God, through the gifts of the Holy Spirit given at the beginning (at Baptism). This is not to say that the person is called into passivity: it is essential that the person actively cooperate with the Spirit. Yet it is the work of the Spirit that is effective at this time. In the scriptural parallel, between the passion and Pentecost, this was the time when the apostles were hidden, waiting in a room for the most part, and it was the Lord who was the active one. It was their part to receive from Him the inner formation which He was accomplishing.

We should observe that in this stage of formation, the disciples were in the room at prayer with Mary, the mother of the Lord (Ac 1:14). The relationship of a Christian with Jesus Christ changes radically in the illuminative stage: he comes to know the risen Lord! There is another radical change which often occurs in this stage, in the relationship of the Christian with Mary. This is a subject worthy of much attention, but for now we can note that in the illuminative stage, Mary also is known in a new and more intimate way. From the foot of the cross the words of Jesus become piercing and personal.

> Then He said to the disciple, "Behold, your mother!" And from that hour the disciple took her into his own home.   Jn 19:27

The personal experience of the cross, which ushers in the illuminative stage and relationship with the risen Christ, reveals the great dignity of Mary. Before the cross, she was the mother of Jesus, certainly worthy of respect and love. But in the illuminative stage a previously hidden glory begins to emanate from this woman. She is *my* mother! She is the Mother of all the Church! And I take her into my "own home."

The Second Dark Night, and the Unitive Way

Entrance to this stage is less dramatic, in a sense, than that to the other two: it is more hidden and interior; the work of God in the soul is most intimate. This stage is the perfection of what was begun in the illuminative way. The transition to this final stage was accomplished in the apostles with the withdrawal from them of the risen Christ, followed by prayer and waiting "for the promise of my Father." In waiting, in faith and in hope, place was made ready in them for the coming of the Holy Spirit at Pentecost. This, the "third conversion," brought in them the completeness, the perfection, of their formation in Christ. Now they were finally ready to be living witnesses to the Gospel.

In the unitive way the enlightened Christian "lives in a union that is, so to speak, continual with Christ."[25] In the unitive stage the Christian experiences within himself the *life* of the risen Christ: "If then you have been raised with Christ, seek the things that are above, where Christ is, seated at the right hand of God. Set your mind on the things that are above, not on things that are on earth. For you have died, and your life is hid with Christ in God" (Col 3:1-3). The unitive way, Fr. Garrigou-Lagrange writes, is the normal prelude to the beatific vision. In the third stage, an anonymous nun writes that the identification with Christ has become complete: "...they would be ready to die for God and cheerfully; they feel completely detached from the world if they could only gain God. That is the sign of this stage, along with conscious union with His will in daily life; and it is the real test of progress."[26]

Perhaps at the entrance to this stage, or perhaps embodied within it (in the fifth and especially the sixth mansions of St. Teresa) is the very severe trial and purgation of the second dark night, the night of the spirit. We can organize the development of the spiritual life easily and systematically following the historical formation of the apostles by Christ; so doing we would place this dark night of purgation at the ascension, and prior to Pentecost. We are greatly helped in our theological understanding of the spiritual life by doing this, but in the personal lives of souls it is found that this purgation may not be so precisely placed. St. Teresa, recording from her own experience and the experiences of her sisters, placed this most severe purgation in the sixth mansion of spiritual betrothal, near the very summit of the spiritual life.

Conclusion to the Chapter

The three stages of the spiritual journey, then, have been seen and described many times throughout our history. A summary table will help to place in relationship all that we have described so far.

Stages of the Soul:	First Stage	Second Stage	Third Stage
Jesus forms His Disciples:	**Disciples are called, and follow Jesus in His earthly ministry**	**The Passion and Cross; the Forty Days in the Upper Room**	**Ascension; Pentecost: Life in the Spirit**
St. Bernard's Degrees of Charity:	The person discovers God as his greatest good; he serves Him to benefit himself.	The good of God in Himself is seen — he acts in love for God, but still selfishly	God is all; all are loved only in God
St. Thomas Aquinas' Degrees of Charity:	Faith and Baptism: the soul resists sin and seeks grace	The soul grows in virtue and charity	The soul seeks to remain in God
Traditional Catholic Spirituality:	Beginners; Purgative Stage	Proficients; Illuminative Stage	Perfect; Unitive Stage
For comparison — correlation to physical/ emotional growth:	Childhood	Adolescence	Adulthood

The one principle which coheres the three stages of course is Christ, and His life through the Holy Spirit. The goal of the three stages is the perfection of charity, the fulfilling of the law. No matter which stage a Christian is in, his "way" is the same in the sense that his way is Christ. The way is ours to live, in the most personal sense of meaning. Each of us is called to say *yes* to God; each is called to respond with the wholehearted assent of the *I myself* of my being.

More Teachings of Jesus about His Way

Besides the Parable of the Sower, previously discussed, several other teachings of Jesus help us to understand this deeply personal and divine work in us in the three stages of spiritual growth.

1. The Way is of Profound Mystery

> And He said, "The kingdom of God is like a man who scatters seed upon the ground, and sleeps and rises by night and day, and the seed sprouts and grows while he is unaware.
> "The earth bears fruit on its own; first the shoot, then the head of grain, and then the full grain in the head. When it is ripe, he at once sends for the sickle, because the harvest has come."   Mk 4:26-29

The key point here is the necessary mystery to us of our own growth toward God. The kingdom develops, and does so in three stages of growth which can recognized: "first the shoot, then the head, then the full grain in the head." We could understand this today as referring to the three stages: first the purgative stage of the beginner, then the illuminative, then finally the "full grain" of the unitive stage. Yet how does this happen? "He is unaware." This one who does not understand the growth in his field is certainly not God! Rather we are the ones receiving into our own hearts the divinely provided seeds of the kingdom; we are the ones tending our own fields, our own lives. This inherent mystery of our growth is one of the great puzzles of human life and being.

2. The Grace of God is Poured into All His Church

> And again He said, "To what shall I compare the kingdom of God? It is like leaven which a woman took and hid in three measures of flour, til it was all leavened."
>
> Lk 13:20-21

Here we understand that the three measures of flour represent the three stages of relationship with God in the three stages of spiritual development, tended by the woman who is the Church. The saving grace of the Holy Spirit, entrusted to the Church in the Communion of Saints, is here represented by the leaven which enlivens the bread of our self-offering. This grace is active, though hidden, in all three containers of precious flour. All is to be leavened! All will be gathered to the storehouse of the Lord in His kingdom. Yes we are all called to holiness! Yes God intends each one of us to sanctity, to perfection! But it is also true that the grace — that is, the *life* — of God is given to all in His Church: beginner, proficient, and perfect.

3. The Generous Mercy of God Must Not Lead Us to Presumption, or to Complacency

> Then He told this parable: "A man had a fig tree planted in his vineyard; and he came looking for fruit on it and found none.
>
> "So he said to the vinedresser, 'For three years now I have come looking for fruit on this fig tree, and I haven't found any. Cut it down; why should it use up the ground?'
>
> "But in answer the vinedresser said, 'Lord, let it be for this year, too, until I dig around it and put down manure.
>
> "'Maybe it will produce fruit next year; but if it doesn't, have it cut down.'"   Lk 13:6-9

We note here the action of God concerning that fig tree which He has planted: fruitlessness is not acceptable. His response is action on His part: He acts to enable the fruitfulness He desires. We see the three stages again: first the stage of a beginner, the tree with no fruit. Then secondly, the stage of a proficient in which God is the active agent. This is the tree with which God works, beneath the surface so to speak, working the interior soil and infusing the spiritual nutrients of His grace. Finally we see the mature tree, the fruit-bearing stage of the perfect, from which God has every right to expect fruit. Indeed, "Every one to whom much is given, of him will much be required" (Lk 12:48).

Our calling is to the perfection of charity in authentic human life. Each Christian must strive for the perfection of charity: this is the law given to us, in the two great commandments. We are to strive for a life of charity within our stage of Christian formation, and consistent with it, and consistent with our station in life. The charity of a Christian should continue to increase, until his or her death. Fr. Garrigou-Lagrange summarizes and paraphrases many of the fathers of the Church, "In the way of salvation, he who does not advance, goes back." "If life does not ascend, it descends."[27]

Notes

[1] St. Thomas, *Summa*, IIa, IIae, q.184, a.1.

[2] Reginald Garrigou-Lagrange, O.P., *The Three Ages of the Interior Life*, trans. M. Timothea Doyle, O.P. (Rockford, IL: Tan Books, 1989).

[3] John G. Arintero, O.P., *The Mystical Evolution*, trans. Fr. Jordan Aumann, O.P. (Rockford, IL: Tan Books, 1978).

[4] Jordan Aumann, O.P., *Spiritual Theology* (Allen, TX: Christian Classics, 1980).

[5] Reginald Garrigou-Lagrange, O.P., *Christian Perfection and Contemplation*, trans. M. Timothea Doyle, O.P. (St. Louis: B. Herder, 1954), 159.

[6] Ibid., 160.

[7] Garrigou-Lagrange, O.P., *The Three Ages of the Interior Life*, vol. 1, 230-238.

[8] Ibid., 249-252.

[9] Garrigou-Lagrange, O.P., *Christian Perfection and Contemplation*, 161.

[10] St. Thomas, *Summa*, II, II, q.184, a.3.

[11] St. Thomas, *Summa*, IIa, IIae, q.24, a.9.

[12] St. Bernard of Clairvaux, *The Love of God and Other Writings*, ed. Msgr. Charles Dollen (New York: Alba House, 1996).

[13] St. Bernard of Clairvaux, *The Love of God...*, ch. XV, 1.

[14] Ibid.

[15] Ibid.

[16] Garrigou-Lagrange, O.P., *The Three Ages of the Interior Life*, vol. 1, 229-230.

[17] Ibid.

[18] Ibid.

[19] Ibid., 300.

[20] Garrigou-Lagrange, O.P., *Christian Perfection and Contemplation*, 9-10.

[21] A Discalced Carmelite Nun, *The Stages of Prayer* (St. Paul, MN: Carmel of Our Lady of Divine Providence, 1971), 2.

[22] Benedict J. Groeschel, C.F.R., *Spiritual Passages* (New York: Crossroad, 1998), 82.

[23] There is no contradiction between St. Teresa and the Discalced Carmelite of note 21, if we understand that many souls enter the door of Illumination in the first night, but most fail to persevere through its trials. These fall back to the beginning stage.

[24] St. Teresa of Avila, *Interior Castle*, Trans. E. Allison Peers (Garden City, NY: Image Books, 1961), 94.

[25] Garrigou-Lagrange, O.P., *Christian Perfection and Contemplation*, 10.

[26] A Discalced Carmelite Nun, 9.

[27] Garrigou-Lagrange, O.P., *Christian Perfection and Contemplation*, 189.

CHAPTER THREE

GROWING INTIMACY
WITH CHRIST: SCRIPTURE

Listening to Holy Scripture

The Bible — the Holy Scripture — is rightly called the Word of God not only because it is His expression: that is, God is the primary author of Scripture. The Bible is also rightly called the Word of God because it is an authentic self-revelation of God. Prayerful listening to Scripture opens us to hear not only words about God, and not only words from God. Prayerful listening to Scripture opens us to hear God Himself.

How do we prayerfully listen to Scripture? This chapter is intended to help us approach the Bible as we ought, and as we must if we would truly hear it. Mere facts and even Church teachings about the Bible are in themselves inadequate to this intention. Listening techniques are in themselves insufficient. Theological ideas about hearing and believing, true though they may be, may not be sufficient to open a human heart to the living presence of God speaking. Yet this intercourse with the divine can occur! A human soul can be lifted up to the sacred, and can "hear" in some spiritual way the eternal self-expression of God, the Person Jesus Christ. "So faith comes from what is heard, and what is heard comes through the word of Christ" (Rm 10:17).

Holy Scripture is given to us as a means of grace. It is a help for us in our life-journey to sacred relationship with Christ and sacred fellowship in the Trinity. Through Scripture as well as through other means, the Person of the Holy Spirit actively works in human persons to gather us into Christ. This gathering into Christ, as we have seen, occurs in stages of spiritual growth. The three stages of our incorporation into Christ will be seen from different perspectives in this chapter, all referenced however to the Holy Scripture, the Bible.

The Person of the Holy Spirit is essential to our understanding of Scripture. Apart from the living activity of the Spirit in a listening soul, Scripture presents us with mere words. With the Spirit, however, a soul can hear and understand. In Scripture, the Holy Spirit inspired men to write all that God willed, and only those things He willed.[1] The Church assures us that Scripture was written under the inspiration of the Holy Spirit, and therefore "must be read and interpreted with its divine authorship in mind" if it is to be truly heard, and rightly understood.[2]

In the chapter before this one, the three stages of spiritual growth in holiness were found in Scripture in the formative method of Christ Himself. Jesus made Christians of His followers, He formed them into disciples and saints, following the pattern of spiritual development we now describe in the three stages.

In this chapter, we will see these stages prefigured in the time even before Christ — in the divinely prescribed designs of both tabernacle and temple. We will also see these stages manifest today, in the ministry of the Holy Spirit gathering the Church into Christ as she listens and prays the Holy Scripture.

That is, we will see these stages reflected in the ever present "voice" of the Holy Spirit in the Bible, in what tradition calls the three spiritual senses of Scripture. Finally, we will consider methods of listening which can help us to understand Him and to cooperate with His work in us, in the three stages of our own spiritual development.

In this chapter I hope to encourage fellow Christians to integrate the prayer and study of Scripture into their lives. The Bible must be approached with reverence, with a profound conviction of the unique and sacred character of the work. For personal encounter to occur, that is, for there to be an encounter of a human person with God, the human person must bring to the encounter *himself*. We cannot come to the Bible withholding some part of ourselves.

Praying Scripture

To pray Scripture is more than reverent listening, as essential and important as that is. To pray Scripture is to be present to the Word. It is to be with Him in His loving word to us as persons. This requires focus, and concentration, and attentiveness, and patience — yet all this does not convey the full meaning of one person being present to Another. To pray Scripture requires reverent listening and the active engagement of the mind, with a waiting and obedient heart. Becoming personally present to the Word is not instantly accomplished: a learning process is involved.

How to begin? Most of us are not prepared to read the Word of God as He deserves! Our training in reading has been typically ordered to anything but reverence. We read in school for tests, developing the art of anticipating the questions of our teachers. We read casually for entertainment and pleasure, as scarce time permits, scanning and skipping around as we freely choose. We read for business and profit, culling through the words for whatever seems of value to us here and now. Words for us are seen as information for our profit, or entertainment for our pleasure.

Rarely do we have the sense of words as treasure of infinite value, or of food for life in a time of famine, or of clear and clean water in a parched, dead-dry desert. Yet the Word of God, in Scripture, is all this and more. His words to us are living seed, with potentials for full growth that we cannot imagine. His words are healing medicine to dying mankind. His words are boundless wealth to the destitute poor, and rejuvenation to those broken by age. His words are all this and more, because they are His word to us, His children whom He loves with a love we can hardly begin to grasp. Scripture speaks to us as words and thoughts having power within themselves. In the beginning, the word of God "Let there be light!" *caused* light to *be*. This is the power of the Word of God, to which we listen: words with the power to *cause* human transformation, yet awaiting our free cooperation.

A mere scholar, in the narrow and academic sense of the word, will not meet God in the controlled arena of his intellect, if he presents this and only this in his seeking. But similarly, a person who withholds his mind and his intellect, who does not offer his understanding to the revealed truth of God, but seeks only maxims and rules of obedience, will not meet God in His Word. We cannot meet God on our terms, opening some areas of our lives to Him while refusing His presence in other areas. Seeking God impersonally, or conditionally, can lead us only to idols of our own making. We must seek Him as persons: we must be available to Him personally, with minds and hearts and lives present, listening, waiting. The Bible is an essential help for personal spiritual growth, for rightly knowing both God and ourselves.

Catholics and the Bible

The easy availability of the Bible to us today is a great blessing. Bibles are inexpensive, and accurate, readable translations are at hand. All Catholics are urged by the leaders of the Church to a careful and prayerful listening to Holy Scripture. In spite of all this, many Catholics in contemporary America are shamefully ignorant of the Bible. Many even think of the Bible as a "Protestant" book, or at least one that only Protestants would read. Catholics hear Scripture readings at Mass, but many of us will never take the time for personal and private reading of this great treasure. Many Catholics have difficulty identifying or even locating individual books of the Bible. Many are woefully ignorant of major biblical themes, historical events, and important parables of our Lord.

Considering that the Bible is truly the book of the Catholic Church, our current neglect of it should be especially embarrassing. This neglect is certainly not officially sanctioned or taught, but for many years it was, sadly, allowed without much exhortation to the contrary. In fairness to Catholics, however, we need to consider the whole history of this problem. It is true that the Bible was given into the care of the Catholic Church. The sons of the Church were inspired by the Holy Spirit to write the sacred revelations of God. The Church, by the inspiration of the same Holy Spirit, recognized the truth of these special works, and guarded them as sacred. She separated them from the many other "gospels" and writings which were circulated among the churches in the early days; she collected the authentic revelations of God into the official canon of the Church. This Bible was carefully protected and passed on through the generations and the centuries. It was and is our sacred book, the very Word of God.

The reading and the interpretation of this treasure of the

Church was always understood to be possible only within the faith of the Church. Uncovering the full meaning of God's Word for humanity, that is, authentic biblical interpretation, was always recognized within the Church as the responsibility of the Church herself. Specifically, the right interpretation of Scripture, and not only the ordinary devotional reading of it, was guaranteed by Christ Himself to His Church. His trustworthy truth would be passed on from within the body of the apostles whom He personally sent, and through them authority was passed on to their successors the bishops. In this way, the Church was to be protected from erroneous readings of the Scripture by the abiding presence of His Spirit among us. Thus the hierarchy of the Church, as successors of the apostles, are the authoritative interpreters of His Word.

In the Protestant Reformation, however, private interpretations of Scripture were preached and taught as true, even when they contradicted the understandings and meanings which were held as authentic by the Church. Understandings of meanings of Scripture which had been held by the Church for fifteen hundred years were now cast aside and replaced by new understandings that seemed better to the sixteenth century minds of the reformers. Newly arrived at and privately formed interpretations, independent of the mind of the Church, independent of the wisdom of fifteen centuries, were offered to reform congregations. Private interpretation of the Bible, a license which is contrary to the very purpose and origin of the Bible, was proclaimed as a basic right and a new norm of reformed Christianity. The result has been the unbridled proliferation of sects, denominations, and false interpretations of God's Word.

The Catholic Church became understandably cautious, and even more careful to guard the truth of Scripture against both untrained laity and undisciplined clergy who might pervert the holy and precious revelation of the Word. A sad consequence of the defensive "fortress mentality" which became established in the Church was an overly cautious protectiveness. Many in the laity were not encouraged to, and were sometimes discouraged from, personal familiarity with Scripture. The Bible became seen as a dangerous book, better left to the experts. This overreaction within the Church was very clearly repudiated by Vatican II which, to the contrary, returned to Scripture the place in Christian life it was always intended to have.

Brothers and Sisters in Christ

Before leaving the subject of the Reformation, however, something must be said to forbid any sense of animosity toward our Protestant brothers and sisters. The break in the unity of the Church, in the so-called "Reformation," was a grievous event in our history. Schism is a real tragedy for many reasons, and is an insult to the dignity and reputation of God among human persons. The saving Gospel of Christ is confused and clouded by the divisions among those who profess "one Lord, one faith, one baptism" (Eph 4:5).

We, however, must realize and choose to live in the tender love of Christ for all the children of God. We must share His fervent desire for our unity, our re-gathering in love. Authentic ecumenism, without compromising with the truth of God in any way, is at the very heart of Vatican II.

The true Church of Christ does indeed subsist in the Catholic Church. Yet there are elements of truth outside of her visible structures,[3] specifically within Protestant churches, and these must be respected and honored. These elements of truth have their home in the Catholic Church, and so they are actually factors which tend toward our reunion. We are called to look upon Protestant Christians as our real brothers and sisters, offering to them authentic fraternal love. At the same time, we Catholics must be careful to preserve our fidelity to the whole revealed truth of Christ, while doing what we can to work for our eventual reunion in Him.

To understand Protestant views of the Bible, we must begin by acknowledging the reverence they give it. Our Protestant brothers and sisters recognize the Bible as the Word of God, as indeed it is. They give it a place of primacy in their worship, both private and public, which honors God in His Word and should draw praise from all Christians. We read in *The Word, Church, and Sacraments in Protestantism and Catholicism*, written by a Catholic even before the Vatican II exhortations toward ecumenism,

> Living Protestantism takes its life from its understanding of the Bible in the light of the spirit who gave it. Only when we acknowledge this can we understand all that the Bible means to Protestants, how it is and always will be for them a living source of genuine spirituality.

The author, Louis Bouyer, Cong. Orat., continues, "we must unhesitatingly recognize that it [Protestant worship] is basically an effort to restore Christian worship to what it was in the beginning."[4] This "Protestant" spirituality which comes from genuine devotion to God's Word is of course part of *Catholic* tradition. Devotion to Scripture originated in our Church, and belongs here. The place that Scripture should occupy in the lives of Catholics was reasserted in the Second Vatican Council, which recalled the simple but profound statement of St. Jerome, "Ignorance of the Scriptures is ignorance of Christ."[5]

The Council devoted one of the four solemn Constitutions to the Word of God. This important document, *Dei Verbum*, recognizes the importance of Scripture in the life of the Church. We place the Bible alongside the most Holy Eucharist as our true bread of life: the Church "unceasingly receives and offers to the faithful the bread of life from the table both of God's Word and of Christ's body."[6] The Eucharist itself, the sacrament of Christ Himself, is given the very highest place of honor in the Church as "the source and summit of the Christian life."[7]

The Council fathers clearly want devotion to Scripture to grow in the Church. We read, "Just as the life of the Church is strengthened through more frequent celebration of the Eucharistic mystery, similarly we may hope for a new stimulus for the life of the Spirit from a growing reverence for the Word of God, which lasts forever."[8] Finally, the Council gives high praise to the holy Word as both source and food for the spiritual life:

> All the preaching of the Church must be nourished and regulated by Sacred Scripture. For in the sacred books, the Father who is in heaven meets His children with great love and speaks with them; and the force and power in the Word of God is so great that it stands as the support and energy of the Church, the strength of faith for her son, the food of the soul, the pure and everlasting source of spiritual life.[9]

We need holy Scripture to grow and to become formed in Christ. Scripture keeps us balanced and grounded in a healthy self-knowledge, as well as bringing us the inspired revelation of God. Scripture is the reliable testimony of faithful witnesses, of God's work among us to return us to His original intention. The use of "us" in this description is intentional: we belong together; we share a vocation and a destiny. All of humanity is one family, created by the one God, intended for and invited to divine fellowship in the Holy Trinity.

Return, Through a Chosen People

In the first few chapters of Genesis, Scripture recounts our fall from original grace. In the remainder of the Bible, we read of God's mighty hand and His sacrificial heart at work to restore the family of humanity to His plan, which is a sharing in His divine love. There was an original "place of meeting" in the Garden of Eden: humanity and God could have fellowship together, and they did. But man did not remain faithful to the relationship God offered him. Man rebelled in his freedom, and separated himself from goodness and truth, and caused a wall of division even within himself.

Man was now fallen to an anxious essential loneliness, yet God would not abandon His creation or His original intention. God would work with man, even in his confused condition, and would patiently draw man back to Himself. Like a loving Father, God would reclaim His prodigal family as His own.

We learn in the history of salvation of a chosen people. It is important to understand how and why God could choose one people apart, out of His whole created humanity. This understanding is important for us today as a Church, because God has not changed. The love extended by God is universal! God does not love one people more than another, but He works among people differently to show His universal love. The Church is the chosen people of the New Covenant, and this has definite implications for every member of His Church. As we come to understand God's work in a chosen people, we will come to understand the divine burden which Christ left for us.

God works for the salvation of all mankind by choosing and especially blessing some, leaving need in others, so that all might live interdependently. In this way divine charity is encouraged among persons. In this way human persons have the opportunity to participate in divine love. Therefore God chose one people among all the nations, as His chosen people. He called Abram to walk in special obedience, promising that he would be a blessing for all the nations of mankind (Gn 22:18). This chosen people would suffer many hardships in their formation under the hand of God, but He was working in them in order to work through them for all mankind. This might not be the way that we would choose, but it is God's way: He chooses some, to be a blessing for all. He showed this to perfection in His incarnation as man, Jesus Christ. Christ suffered much, pouring Himself out as a love offering, not for Himself but for all of us. He is then our model of Christian perfection, and specifically our model for the Christian journey toward the perfection of charity. His love was demonstrated to us at the cross; we are all called to take up our crosses, and follow Him (Mt 16:24 ff.).

Rebuilding the Meeting Place

The early history of the chosen people, seen in the life-story of Abram, demonstrates our journey of return to God, to find again that lost "meeting place" where human persons could have fellowship with God. This history also demonstrates the transience of our walk on this earth. Transience is again a theme in the Exodus in the wilderness, journeying toward the Promised Land. In all their wanderings, as in all our wanderings, God is with His people. While they dwelt in tents in the wilderness, so He dwelt among them in a tent, in His tabernacle. In this way the human hope for return to our true and complete "meeting place" with God would be kept alive. Later, when the time was right, He would establish them as a nation Israel, as a kingdom under David to be "established forever." God was working, moving us toward His intention.

Through David He would establish His house, to be built by the descendant of David. In a revealing use of double meaning to David, the Lord declared "your house and your kingdom shall stand firm forever before Me" (2 S 7:16). David, in the zeal of his heart, wanted to build a house for the Lord as a holy temple, but the Lord declared to him that no, it would be the other way around: God would build the house of David! It is one of the beautiful and joyful surprises of Scripture that these two "buildings" (both as nouns and as verbs) coincide. The house (or household, family line) of David would be the house (temple, meeting place) of God, established forever by the descendant of David according to the flesh, Jesus Christ.

It is significant also to note that for both of God's dwelling places, for both the tabernacle and the temple, the house was of God's explicit design and pattern. God gave Moses the specific design of the tabernacle in the wilderness (Ex 25:9): "According to all that I show you concerning the pattern of the tabernacle, and of all its furniture, so you shall make it." And when the time was right to establish kingdom and temple, again the specific pattern was given by God to a man, to David (1 Ch 28:19), which was then passed on to his son Solomon (vs. 11).

We can begin to see in part the revelation of God's work. God Himself made the first place of meeting, the garden Eden, which Adam and Eve spurned in sinful independence and self-centered preference for the things of creation. The pattern and design for God's meeting with mankind would be kept in God's hands, in the heavenly places, but God began to allow man to build with Him, to build a place of meeting for them. God wanted fellowship with human persons, creatures who had been made in God's own image and likeness, but mankind was estranged and confused in his sin. Change was needed, and God acted. The reformation of humanity and our return to God was displayed, by design, through God's chosen people. The worship which God's people the Jews were chosen to demonstrate first to themselves and then to the whole world, began His revelation of the path to holiness.

The Three Stages of the First Covenant

The tabernacle and later the temple had three major physical divisions of space. There was an outer court, then an enclosed sanctuary which was itself divided into two spaces. First was the holy place, then the holiest place, the Holy of Holies.[10] The outer court could be accessed by those belonging to the covenant of Israel; the holy place, by the priests of the tribe of Levi (Nb 8:14 ff.); the Holy of Holies, only by the high priest and only once a year on the Day of Atonement.

These stages of approach to the holiest place, where ultimately God Himself was present to His people through the mediation of the high priest, were later revealed (in Scripture in the Letter to the Hebrews) to be only a pattern of the heavenly reality made complete by Christ.

> But when Christ came as the high priest of the good things that have come, He passed through the greater and more perfect tent which is not made by human hands (that is, it is not part of this creation), and entered once for all into the sanctuary bearing

His own blood rather than the blood of rams and
bullocks, and thus secured for us an eternal redemption.   Heb 9:11-12

Now everyone has access to the sanctuary, the holiest place,
the Holy of Holies. Now the return to fellowship with God is
possible, because of Jesus Christ. Now, "through the blood of
Jesus we have the confidence to enter the sanctuary by the new
and living way He opened for us... that is, the way of His flesh"
(Heb 10:19).

This Letter to the Hebrews does not imply, however, that
the journey to genuine intimacy with God can now be accomplished in a single step because of Jesus. Rather, all believers
are exhorted to grow toward the perfecting of that which they
have received. Jesus is "the pioneer and perfecter of our faith"
(Heb 12:2). We must strive to remain faithful, to cleanse ourselves, to pursue holiness of life, and to live the love of Christ.
It is interesting that after establishing the doctrine that the way
is indeed now open to us all (and therefore all are called to this
holiness), we are warned of the corresponding obligation to live
a holy life. We read, "if, after receiving knowledge of the truth,
we sin deliberately, there no longer remains a sacrifice for sins.
What remains instead is the fearful prospect of judgment" (Heb
10:26-27).

The book of Hebrews goes on to devote a chapter to re-
counting the heroic faith of the saints, therefore encouraging
us to persevere. This eleventh chapter is the kind of exhortation appropriate to the purgative stage. The next chapter, the
twelfth, calls us to patient endurance under the hand of God's
discipline, and the patient pursuit of sanctification. This chapter twelve is then highly and especially appropriate to those
entering the illuminative stage through the dark night of pas-

sive purgations, and to those already in it who are seeking to grow in virtue. Chapter thirteen begins with, "Let brotherly love continue," with encouragement to solidarity with all those suffering in the Church. These and other exhortations in the chapter are especially appropriate to those in the unitive stage, those called in one form or another to a complete self-giving in love for the Church in the name of Christ. We read,

> Therefore Jesus too suffered outside the gate in order to sanctify the people with His own blood. So let us go out to Him outside the camp and share the abuse He bore.   Heb 13:12-13

These last exhortations prepare us for the sacrificial attitude of the stage of the perfect, the attitude in fact of martyrs.

The three stages of approach to God were prefigured outwardly in the design of the tabernacle, and again in the temple. First there was the outer court, then the holy place, then the Holy of Holies. This corresponds to our personal and interior journey: first the purgative stage, then the illuminative, then the unitive. Our return, after the tragic break because of sin, finally would be made possible by God Himself in the Person of the Son. In Baptism we are in fact incorporated *into* Him, brought to the meeting place with God in a way fallen humanity could never have foreseen. In Christ we are infused with the supernatural virtues of faith, and hope, and charity: each virtue revealing something specific to each of the three stages. Yet Baptism and these virtues which order us to a share in the life of God do not instantly raise us to the maturity of life in Him. Patient endurance and cooperation with grace are required of us. We are called, as were the apostles, to remain in Him who is both the author and perfecter of our faith.

Word and Spirit in Soul Formation

Scripture is the Word of God. When we say this, we are not saying that the written words are identical with the Son of God, who is rightly called *the* Word (John 1). It is true that some people have what is near to an idolatrous stance toward the Bible, and even to some translations of the Bible in particular. The Bible is worthy of the greatest reverence, but we do not worship the Bible nor do we try to read it in a rigid and literalistic way.

The Bible is a work both of humanity and of God, and the interpretation of the Bible requires that we read it in this light. The human side of its authorship admits of human investigation, which has received great attention in recent years. Such investigation is now called modern critical study, and has deepened the scriptural understanding of the Church in many ways. Modern critical study alone, however, is inadequate to a complete understanding of Scripture, because it is also true that God is the author of Scripture. The Bible must be read and understood in the Spirit, that is, in the same Holy Spirit who inspired the writing of it.

The Bible cannot be understood apart from the Spirit who is the life-principle of its writing. The Holy Spirit moved certain members of the Church, the Body of Christ, to record words and meanings intended by God to be passed on to the whole Church. The Bible is then a communication of God to His Church, and must be listened to with the mind of the Church. That is, apart from the Church the Bible is out of context. Within the Church, the Spirit is the life-principle moving meaning from the sacred text to the human heart. The Spirit brings life to the Body, from the mind and heart of God.

When we listen to Scripture, we must listen with faith. We are listening to God, within the Church which is the Body of the Son still on earth. He wants to bless us and upbuild us. He wants to give us wisdom, so that we might be a blessing to all the nations. He wants us to have a part in His work of re-gathering. He wants to draw us to the very perfection of charity, "to unity of faith and knowledge of the Son of God, to mature manhood, to the extent of Christ's full stature" (Eph 4:13).

The Spiritual Senses of Scripture

Divine revelation to humanity possesses layers or dimensions of meaning. Scripture has been recognized, in Catholic tradition, to have four senses of meaning: the literal sense, and three different spiritual senses. The historical or literal sense is that intended in the meanings of the words themselves. There also may exist a less obvious but divinely intended spiritual sense in a given passage consistent with that foundational literal sense. Under the heading of spiritual sense, tradition finds three properly called spiritual senses: the allegorical, the moral (or tropological), and the anagogical. The complete four senses are briefly described in *The Catechism of the Catholic Church*,[11] and more fully by St. Thomas Aquinas in his commentary on Galatians.[12]

Tradition reaching back to John Cassian has recognized these senses. For example, the word "Jerusalem" has the literal meaning of the earthly city of that name. There are also spiritual meanings that can be heard. The place "Jerusalem," in certain contexts and circumstances, can carry the allegorical meaning of the Church to come through Christ. "Jerusalem" can also carry a moral sense: moral imperatives for the Christian today, of the faithfulness we are to live and the hardheartedness we are to avoid. "Jerusalem" also can carry anagogical meaning, signifying the heavenly city to come at the end of time. These three traditionally recognized spiritual senses of Scripture may be seen to correlate with the traditional three stages of personal spiritual growth: the purgative, the illuminative, and the unitive. That is, the Spirit works through revealed Scripture in such a way as to draw the maturing human soul into ever deeper and truer intimacy with God. Particular meanings in Scripture are particularly helpful to souls in the purgative stage. Particular meanings in Scripture are particularly helpful to souls in the illuminative stage. And particular meanings in Scripture are particularly helpful to souls in the unitive stage. Having three spiritual dimensions of meaning, so to speak, the written revelation of God to humanity is a fitting instrument of the divine movements and call within mankind. The Holy Spirit, working within the person to form him and "mature" him in Christ, finds in Scripture the dimensions of meaning especially needed by the particular soul in its particular stage of spiritual life. The Spirit works in the soul of a person, the Word nourishes the soul of the person, all drawing and re-gathering the person back to Christ.

St. Thomas defines the literal meanings in Scripture as "that signification by which the words designate something that pertains to the literal or historical sense." The literal meaning is not the same as the "literalistic" meaning, however. Thomas includes parabolic or metaphorical meanings also under the heading of literal. To say that Jesus sits at the right hand of God is not intended to mean that Jesus literally is sitting in a chair: this is a metaphorical statement, but its metaphorical meaning is included in "the literal meaning" of the passage. The first layer of meaning, so to speak, the literal meaning, is that meaning conveyed by the words themselves as words.

Thomas continues, "But the signification whereby the things signified by the words further signify other things, pertains to the mystical [or spiritual] sense." Thomas observes that Scripture is unique in this, having God as its [primary] author. God is able to have words signify things, as men are able to do when they speak or write. But God is able to go beyond the vocabulary of mankind: He can use things and events in His "vocabulary" to carry meanings, to signify other things as well. These further meanings comprise the spiritual senses within Scripture. By way of example, Thomas discusses the New Law in Christ, and in further explanation, the meanings of the command "Let there be light!"

> However, the mystical or spiritual sense is divided into three types. First, as when the Apostle says that the Old Law is a figure of the New Law. Hence, insofar as the things of the Old Law signify things of the New Law, it is the allegorical sense... the New Law is a figure of future glory. Accordingly, insofar as things in the New Law and in Christ signify things which are in heaven, it is the anagogical sense. Furthermore, in the New Law the things performed by the head are examples of things we ought to do...; this is the moral sense.

> Examples will clarify each of these. For when I say, "Let there be light," referring literally to corporeal light, it is the literal sense. But if it be taken to mean, "Let Christ be born in the Church," it pertains to the allegorical sense. But if one says, "Let there be light," i.e., "Let us be conducted to glory through Christ," it pertains to the anagogical sense. Finally, if it is said "Let there be light," i.e., "Let us be illumined in mind and inflamed in heart through Christ," it pertains to the moral sense.[13]

Scripture reveals Christ in several ways, then. The crossing of the Red Sea was an historical event, but it is also a sign or type of the victory of Christ. The historical fact of the crossing by His people was a communication by God to mankind. This is an example of an allegorical meaning in the scriptural account of the crossing. The many examples of the charitable life of Christ convey more to us than simple historical facts, there is also the sense of what we ought to do. This level of meaning is the moral or tropological sense of the Scripture. There is also eternal significance included in many of the temporal things and events of Scripture, which point us to our true home in God and His eternal kingdom. King David's temple, and the city of Jerusalem, point us to the heavenly Jerusalem which is our destiny. This meaning is included in the anagogical sense of the scriptural passages.

Listening to Scripture

How can we cooperate with the great grace of the Holy Spirit for our growth? How can we open ourselves to His movements within us, in His beautiful self-revelations of Scripture? The answers are simple: we must be *present* to Him; we must *listen* to the Word. In opening the Bible, we are approaching God. We begin from a distance, but we must persevere. We must want closeness to Him. We must listen to His words in order to begin to hear His Word.

The Beginner

We begin in the outer court with the wounded, confused, yet committed soul of a beginner. It is essential that we continue, that we remain with Jesus. Concerning Scripture, this means that we listen and continue to listen. In Scripture the beginner will find food especially for him, as well as mysteries that puzzle and confound him. The Holy Spirit is working to bring the beginner into the presence of the present Christ, and so He will especially grace the listener for this reality. The literal meaning of the events in the life of Christ and the apostles are particularly significant here. The beginner listens, and hears with the beautiful simplicity of a child, of the reality of all that Jesus said and did. Miracles, healings, supernatural powers recorded of Christ — these are no obstacles to the beginner who believes. The grace of faith has gained him entrance to the kingdom. He is not ashamed to be so simple in his faith, assured by the words of Jesus: "Truly I say to you, whoever does not receive the kingdom of God like a child shall not enter it" (Mk 10:15).

The Spirit also provides the beginner great insight into that spiritual sense in Scripture called allegorical. He becomes more and more alert to Christ prefigured throughout the Old Testament. He grows in awareness, if he perseveres, of the presence of Christ in the things and events of scriptural history. He increases in his confident assurance of the presence of Christ throughout all human history: first in promise and in allegory, then in Incarnation, and now in spirit in His Church. All of Scripture becomes the story of Jesus Christ, and it is all wonderful. The beginner is especially graced by the Spirit to find Jesus Christ in Scripture.

The Proficient

The beginner who perseveres, advances. He perseveres with special graces, through the special trials he encounters in

Scripture in the passion of Christ, in life in his own beginnings of participation in the passion. He grows and enters the stage of the proficients, the illuminative stage of spiritual growth. His experience becomes parallel to that of the apostles after the historical passion of Christ, and this stage continues through the apostolic forty days. For the new proficient, this is encounter with Christ in a radically new and different way, parallel to the apostles' encounter with the risen Christ. This time introduces in prayer the first experiences of supernatural contemplation. It is the stage for the Holy Spirit to work an interior moral movement in our hearts, yours and mine, to move us from within toward the intention of God in our creation. In the language of early salvation history, here we are brought into the holy place of the temple.

As the historic and literal holy place of the temple was for the priests alone, so in this "holy place" within Scripture the Christian begins to understand his vocation to be a "heart-priest." Here he begins to perceive *with God* the beauty of sacrifice. The Holy Spirit is now revealing the tropological intention of Holy Scripture. The Christian begins to hear with more and more clarity and simplicity the moral imperative of the life of Christ. Building upon the work of the Spirit in his beginning stage, the Christian experiences this moral imperative not only in the historical example of Jesus, but expanded to include the whole Christ: the whole work of God in salvation history. Having been brought into the *presence* of Christ through the literal and anagogical senses, His eschatological glory begins to show forth in all His days. His passion, and His resurrection, become revealed even in His Incarnation. Here also the passion of Mary can be shared, even from the first when she was told by Simeon, "a sword will pierce your own soul too, so that thoughts of many hearts may be revealed" (Lk 2:35).

The moral or tropological sense of Scripture is revealed

more and differently within the Christian in this illuminative stage. Scripture declares to the interior of the soul from within the heart of revelation what must be done. It is therefore a heart-to-heart revelation. Christ reveals to the Christian, in His Word and through prayer, His will of love.

When God speaks, He can cause according to His will; He can create things. But in sharing Himself, so to speak, in grace, He can cause free human wills to know the interior and personal obligation that accompanies truth. The human soul is moved within by the Spirit, and hears in the Word very personally: Love ought to be lived! This interior transformation is far beyond mere external obedience. In the transforming light of the resurrection, the heart has changed although not yet fully. Christ lives! Hence the whole Christ, the whole Communion of Saints, the whole Church ought also to live! The tropological sense of Scripture is no mere symbolic layer of meaning to be academically described and analyzed, it is the interior enlightenment by the life of Christ.

The Perfect

Scripture tells us that "everyone who asks will receive, and whoever seeks will find, and to those who knock it shall be opened" (Mt 7:8). The beginner did ask, and seek, and knock. With perseverance and the invitation of grace, he discovers himself in the holy place, the illuminative stage, in the presence of the risen Christ. In the presence of the risen Christ he comes to know and to be known by the Holy Spirit. There is however more than the holy place: the Lord desires an even closer relationship. There is the Holy of Holies. More than revealing His sacred wounds to us in His resurrection, He invites us into His passion. More than allowing us into the presence of His sacred heart, He invites us into the interior life of divine charity itself. More in a sense than knowing the Holy Spirit, his very life becomes filled by the Holy Spirit.

The Church is greatly blessed in her saints, those heroic souls who live Christ in genuine and generous devotion. They demonstrate to us radical kingdom-consciousness, and kingdom-living. The saints show us how to live divine charity, and how to respond completely to the graces and the call of God. We can hear the invitation to this sanctity in Scripture, in the anagogical sense of its revelations. Scripture reveals, in a unique way to a soul in the unitive stage, the true center of all created things, all created life, all created time: it is Christ. The perfect soul does not merely conclude that Christ is the absolute center of creation, nor even does he merely see it in some impersonal way. This is rather the most personal of truths, the most urgent of revelations. He knows that he is in Christ, and Christ is in him; his life is Christ, and the life of Christ is his. The sacred heart of Jesus has opened, and has invited, and has loved this soul. Their hearts have become one. Through Christ, the soul is gathered most intimately into the divinely ordered destiny of the soul: fellowship in the Holy Trinity, the ultimate mystery of mysteries.

Conclusion to the Chapter

Because there is spiritual meaning in Scripture, we cannot read the Bible as if it were any ordinary book. The Bible is not mere history, nor is it merely story, poetry, or myth. We cannot merely analyze it, or speed-read it, or browse through it, or outline and summarize it. But neither can we read the Bible "merely spiritually," certainly not subjectively nor individualistically. The Bible has first of all and foundationally a literal

meaning, and it was intended primarily for a community of believers. Within the foundation of its literal meaning, and to the
faith-community of the Church, Scripture unfolds its spiritual
meanings. The Bible is above all a witness to and for the
Church, and must be read within the faith of the Church. Safe
within the faith of the Church, assured by the protection of her
Founder and her Spouse, Christ truly reveals Himself in His
word. We must therefore guard ourselves against the self-centered individualism of our times, and look always to the generous personalism of our Christian calling. Within real human
sharing, in the relatedness with one another which we were
made for — that is, within the authentic truth and love of Christ
in His Church — we are in the right environment to listen.

The key to listening to Scripture is *listening*. The words
of Scripture carry truth to our hearts, the very truth we hunger
for and need. "So faith comes from what is heard, and what is
heard comes through Christ's word" (Rm 10:17). A way to characterize the right approach to reading or listening to Scripture
is to say we need to pray Scripture. Understanding of the meaning of this awaits a fuller development of prayer itself, which
follows in the next chapter. At this point, however, we anticipate that prayer must surely reflect one's relationship with God,
and so would follow the traditional stages of spiritual growth.

Three Stages of Listening

The results of prayerful listening to Scripture, whatever
the method or process employed, will reflect the depth and intimacy of personal covenant with God. For the person in the
beginning stage, for the person in the illuminative stage, and
for the person in the unitive stage the encounter with God will
be consistent with their relationship with Him. All will be *lis-*

tening, but the hearing will depend upon the "ears to hear" which each brings. Scripture presents three different spiritual senses of meaning; we the Church bring three different hearers to the listening. All are needful; all will be fed.

Beginners, in need of repentance and purgation, will find in Scripture the promise and the presence of Christ our salvation. Through allegory and prophecy in the Old Testament, through the literal meaning in the New, Christ is made present and the word of salvation and renewal is heard. Through listening, the beginner hears the reality now of Christ, for us and in us.

The proficients in the illuminative stage will find in Scripture the presence of Christ the supernatural and resurrected One: that light who illumines us. Not only in the express moral teachings of Jesus, but more powerfully in the example of the life of Christ, is the imperative heard: this is how we are to live. This is the same Christ who was read of in the beginning stage; His moral teachings and His life are the same. The ears — the heart — of the listener, however, are now different. Resurrection faith, and resurrection life, are now awakened and enlivened. The life of Christ finds now in the hearer not only the imperatives of "should" and "ought to do," but the resonances of "want to do." The words of the Bible are the same words; the Word, the Christ, is heard differently in a soul transformed to this deeper stage of relationship in Him.

In the unitive stage, those living martyrs who are the perfect in Christ are living their personal expression of His divine and human example. Their hearing of Scripture resonates with their own personal living Christian expression. He is their perfection, as they are His completion. Their lives exhibit the kingdom of God for us all. They are our beloved saints. They are living Bibles, living testimonies to His Word, living models of the Christian truth. Scripture becomes a language of explanation of their lives, a means of our understanding them. Who are they? What are they doing? Why do they live this way? Holy Scripture explains them, because the reason for them is Jesus Christ.

Notes

[1] Vatican II, *Dei Verbum*, 11.

[2] *Dei Verbum*, 12.

[3] Vatican II, *Lumen Gentium,* 8.

[4] Louis Bouyer, Cong. Orat., *The Word, Church, and Sacraments in Protestantism and Catholicism* (New York: Desclee Company, 1961), p. 23.

[5] St. Jerome, *Comm. In Isaias*, Prol.: *PL* 24, 17; cf. *Dei Verbum,* 25.

[6] *Dei Verbum,* 21.

[7] *Lumen Gentium,* 11.

[8] *Dei Verbum,* 26.

[9] *Dei Verbum,* 21.

[10] Cf. Heb 9; Ex 25 ff.

[11] *Catechism of the Catholic Church*, 115-119.

[12] Thomas Aquinas, *Commentary on Saint Paul's Epistle to the Galatians*, trans. F.R. Larcher, O.P. (Albany, NY: Magi Books, 1966), 138.

[13] Ibid.

CHAPTER FOUR

GROWING IN HOLINESS: PRAYER

Growing Intimacy in Prayer

God has called us to holiness. This word cannot be understood except within the love of God. Outside of God's love, in the world of guilt, self-condemnation and isolation, "holiness" is only another impossible demand. In our sin, "holiness" mocks us and if it is presumptuously claimed, we lie to ourselves and to others. Like humility, holiness is an attribute of God found only in Him and never apart from Him.

God alone is holy; He is true to His own nature, truth itself. Our holiness is by having part in Him: in His truth, His love. Primarily and crucially, our vocation is into the *life* of God, which means into His *love*. Our call to holiness must be understood within our call into relationship with God. Only in holiness of life do we find personal relationship with Him, not because He then rewards our achievement of human effort! Rather, in relatedness to Him, within communion, within companionship with Him, there is holiness by virtue of *His life.*

Prayer, inseparable from holiness, also must be understood in reference to relationship. Seen within a journey to holiness, prayer is both an essential means to that end, and also

83

an indicator of our progress. Seen within a relationship of deepening love, prayer is also both essential means and indicator. Considered from the human side, prayer is simply communication with God. In our journey toward God we need this communication which reveals God to us and also reveals the condition of our relationship. Prayer is not merely "talking to God," it is talking with God.

Considered not only "from the human side" but within the perspective of relationship, *divine relatedness* within the Holy Trinity, prayer is revealed as more. Jesus prayed! The Son, Second Person of the Trinity, in His human condition through the Incarnation, prayed to His Father and our Father. Prayer now, since Jesus, must be understood in the light of Jesus in prayer to our Father. The eternal and divine love-communion between Father and Son was brought into the human condition, in human flesh and voice, because Jesus prayed. Because we are *in Him*, by grace, we enter by our prayer into His prayer. Because of Him, we are as close to the Father as John the Beloved Disciple was to Jesus, as he rested his head upon His sacred breast and upon His sacred heart. We are even closer than John was physically, because we are where he was spiritually, when by grace we pray *in Him*.

Prayer is personal: a person-to-Person encounter with Absolute Truth. Far more than an occasion of whispering into the darkness, or of talking to ourselves, it is an occasion for both listening and learning with God. This listening and learning occurs as we pray verbally, as we pray silently, and as we pray passively receiving the cleansing touches of our Lord. Prayer becomes the embrace of Truth, when we make ourselves His own, and Himself our own. Then prayer becomes the means for the incarnation of Truth, as we live Truth in this creation.

Our desire for communication with God grows, as we grow nearer to Him. As the soul progresses and develops through the stages of the spiritual life to the perfection of charity, then our prayer changes. This chapter describes the stages of prayer which the soul can experience in its journey to God, as it moves through the stages of intimacy with God characterized by the three: the stages of the beginner, the proficient, and the perfect.

There is not complete agreement on the characterization of the stages of prayer, nor on exactly how the stages of deepening prayer fit with the generally agreed upon three stages of the spiritual life. But the points of disagreement are minor. The uncertainty arises in how exactly to place the almost definitive descriptions of prayer given by St. Teresa of Avila in her seven mansions of the soul, with the traditionally accepted three spiritual stages. The clear presentation of prayer given by Fr. Aumann, and the reasonable and workable correlation of her mansions with the spiritual stages given by Fr. Garrigou-Lagrange will be adopted here.

Prayer as Love-Communication

Because He is the true Bridegroom of our souls, our relationship with God has natural analogies in the love relationship between a man and a woman. It is not untrue to liken our prayer with God to the communication between man and woman, as their relationship grows and deepens in love, finally to consummation and fruitfulness in marriage. For two human persons, the intimacy of their relationship is revealed and demonstrated by the nature of their conversation. Whether formal and distant, or simple and trusting, whether centered in the head, or centered in the heart, whether essentially verbal or an essentially wordless embrace, the communication characterizes the relationship. Yet all relationships must begin in distance and separation. Prayer too begins with distance and formality, but as the relationship grows, the prayer will show change to increasing intimacy.

Even in growing intimacy with human persons, God remains always God. He is eternal and absolute, and never is "reduced" merely to a too-familiar friend. Prayer must never be so casual as to be superficial, and we never become presumptuous toward the Almighty. Yet in heartfelt sincerity we grow closer and closer, moving ever deeper into His loving heart. In the deepest and most profound human unions of love, we should never see trust and faithfulness degenerate into presumption or careless disrespect. Growing and loving intimacy rather is accompanied by growing respect and appreciation for the dignity of the other person. A genuine reverence is appropriate to all love, even between human persons, because we are made in the divine image. So also in prayer, a holy fear of God is never absent in even the highest saints, in their deepest prayer. This is not the fear of judgment, which true love casts out (1 Jn 4:18); it is reverence, a virtue which is fitting and beautiful.

Systematic Stages of Prayer

There are two major stages or types of prayer, called (1) ascetical prayer, and (2) mystical prayer. The difference between these two is radical. These two types of prayer differ not in degree but in kind, and in essence. Ascetical prayer includes types of prayer that are more usual, with which we are more familiar. Ascetical prayer is prayer that we are capable of initiating and doing, with ordinary grace. Mystical prayer is more unusual; it is prayer that we are not capable of initiating or doing with ordinary grace. Mystical prayer is a communication with human persons which is initiated by God, which we are especially graced to receive and experience.

Where ascetical prayer can be thought of as our work, mystical prayer is God's work in the soul. In mystical prayer our active cooperation is required, but our active initiation can not cause it. Mystical prayer is something God does to us: it is His communication and His work within us. The beginning of mystical prayer, which is called infused contemplation, is so radically different from any previous prayer experience that it is unmistakably of God.

A person who wonders whether he has had an experience of mystical prayer has probably not, and one who feels certain that he has had such an experience still possibly has not. We can be deceived, and we can deceive ourselves. A strong subjective sense is not a guarantee of the objective spiritual reality, but the objective spiritual reality is undeniable and unforgettable. Also, mystical prayer itself is not the same as unusual "mystical experiences" such as visions, locutions, and other extraordinary spiritual occurrences. Such spiritual experiences can have their origin in human nature or even in the evil spirit, and not necessarily in God. An eager soul with imagination who wants to grow in the spiritual life can possibly unconsciously fabricate experiences, and thereby confuse himself. Discernment of unusual spiritual experiences is obviously very important; the counsel of a wise spiritual director is recommended for help if such experiences come.

STAGES WITHIN ASCETICAL PRAYER

Vocal Prayer

Ascetical prayer is the first type of prayer we ordinarily experience. This initial kind of conversation may, with perseverance and the grace of God, lead into the deeper and more intimate relationships of mystical prayer. Ascetical prayer itself has several stages, which differ in degree of spiritual relationship more than in kind. One way to characterize the stages within ascetical prayer is through use of the terms vocal prayer, meditation, affective prayer, and the prayer of simplicity.[1]

Vocal prayer, the "elementary" stage of ascetical prayer, is foundational and must not be neglected. This is any verbal prayer, written or spoken, formula or spontaneous. This type of prayer is the ordinary entrance into prayer communication with God. It is the kind of prayer used in public gatherings and liturgy, and it is the first "way" of praying we are taught. Early in catechism classes our children are taught to memorize several important and especially meaningful formula prayers, which are of course vocal prayers: the Our Father, the Hail Mary, the Glory Be, and the Act of Contrition. Our prayer life is intended to grow, as our life of Christian charity grows, but we can never outgrow, so to speak, vocal prayer. We need to know that we can never leave these simple and profound formula prayers, or the liturgical prayer of the Church, behind us!

These are called "formula" prayers, but they must never be reduced to mere outward structures, or thought of as ends in themselves. These formulations of profound spiritual truth are not magic, but are normative of prayer in themselves, and are formative of Christ in us when we pray them rightly. Two requirements exist for rightly prayed vocal prayer: attentiveness of mind, and devotion of heart. It is with the union of both attention and devotion that we present ourselves as whole persons to the Lord. Clearly these characteristics admit of degrees. Our minds can be present in prayer, while our hearts are detached and unaffected. Our hearts can be inflamed with strength of will, and we discover our minds wandering. We have probably all experienced the absence of one or the other or both of them, mind and heart, while praying those formula prayers of the Church that have become all too familiar to us. All of us, the young child, the teen, and adults as well, can admit room for improvement in our prayer life, in the increase of both attention and devotion in vocal prayers.

How do we progress in vocal prayer, increasing both attention and devotion? Obviously, advancement in vocal prayer comes not with mere spontaneity in choice of words over the use of traditional formulas. There is a place for spontaneous verbal prayer, but it is not in itself an improvement over formula prayers. Shallow extemporaneous speeches are not necessarily better than sincerely read prepared talks. Progress in vocal prayer comes with increased attention in truth, and increased devotion in love. This increasing openness to God, in mind and in heart, can come through traditional (formula) prayers of the Church as well as through sincere spontaneous prayer.

There is an advantage to us, in our efforts to advance in the life of prayer, in carefully praying both ways. That is, there is reason to intentionally pray the formula prayers of the Church with careful attention and devotion at appropriate times, and at other times, to seek to grow in spontaneous and sincere personal oral prayer.

When entrusting ourselves to the traditional formula prayers, we can do so with great confidence because there is no question about the orthodoxy of their content. These approved formula prayers — for example the Our Father, the Hail Mary, the Glory Be — come from Truth, and are the truth.

Spontaneous prayer, while possibly very "honest" about our thoughts and feelings, has no guarantee of the truth that may be or not be in them. It can be safer initially to concentrate on established formula prayers, with serious concern to better our attention and devotion in praying them. Later, after having been formed in these normative prayers, it is good and natural to speak spontaneously with the Lord.

Spontaneous Prayer

It becomes, as time progresses, increasingly important to the soul to be *personally present* to the Lord in prayer. The importance of this simple reality, our personal presence, becomes painfully clear when we realize how easy it is in prayer to merely talk to oneself. In formula prayers, we can fall into unconscious recitation; in spontaneous prayer, we can fail to rise above our own interior monologue. Prayer must be more than merely reciting words, and more than talking to oneself! If we are to enter prayer, we must be present to God.

To enter the presence of the Lord, or rather to discover Him, spontaneous prayer is very helpful. In the privacy of a closed room or an open field, speak to God out loud from the reality of your life. Without rehearsal, speak to Him as you would freely speak to a person you can trust. Form into words the feelings, fears, hopes, needs and desires that are pressing for honest expression within you. Speak out to Him and continue to speak until you have said it all. Put it all into words in the presence of God, then wait and listen. God has many ways of speaking to us: in the silence following authentic honesty, we can become aware of His presence *with* us, and His loving response *with* us. In this way, prayer as dialogue is discovered, and the abiding presence of God in human life is experienced.

We must be truthful in our prayer. We must come to God without guile, without pretense, as real human persons. Each of us must come to God as the person he or she in fact is. Consistent with our own honest self-disclosure, we must be open to true self-disclosures from God in response. God can surprise us in this kind of prayer, and can begin to heal us of our idolatries. After pouring out before Him our self-centered desires and shameful preoccupations, we may sense not the condemnations we expect but rather a profound acceptance. Waiting in silence, humbled by the truth, we become aware that He has not abandoned us. "Yes, I know. I know you, and I remain with you. I love you."

Here spontaneous prayer is of great benefit: through brutal honesty with God we come face to face with ourselves, and we come to an experience of His great patience, love and forgiveness. Both of these benefits are necessary to true repentance and conversion, essential components of spiritual growth to holiness.

Praying the Formula Prayers of the Church

Our edifying use of formula prayers, for example the Lord's Prayer, can be greatly helped by an obvious and simple intention: slow down and listen. Slowing down and truly listening to the words we are saying will begin the development of the attention and devotion necessary to fruitful vocal prayer. This is true for all age groups in the Church. Young children, for example, need help in understanding the meanings of the words and phrases they are praying. Some teens, because of weak formation when they were children, may also need basic help with vocabulary. Other teens or adults, having more background and understanding to bring to formula prayers, may need only the encouragement to slow down and listen.

With formula prayers, we must provide time and intention to really listen to what we are praying. This engagement of our minds in prayer, in simply listening more carefully and therefore praying more carefully, has two important results. First, as our minds become enlightened with the beauty of the divine truth of the prayer, our wills — our hearts — are called forth to their proper responses to divine truth, namely devotion and love. That is, attention to truth calls forth the necessary devotion as well. In this way we become sincerely and personally engaged in prayer, and the conditions for fruitfulness in our prayer are in place. Secondly, the engagement of the mind with truth is in itself the beginnings of meditation, the second stage of ascetical prayer. That is, simply paying careful attention in formula vocal prayer lays the groundwork in us for meditation.

Meditation: Light for the Mind

Meditation is the next stage of ascetical prayer, following vocal prayer. Meditation provides the growing need within the soul for divine light, divine truth, in its life of prayer. Adolescents and adults need to see the rationality of their religion. This is a matter which also concerns children, of course, but less so. Children can, without violating their own integrity, completely trust the adults who love and lead them. They are less conscious of the imperfections and contradictions in the lives of adult religious leaders which teens and other adults can be quick to see. Children want and deserve to make sense of the religious truth presented to them, but in the onset of adolescence, this becomes crucial. As we grow into adulthood, the development of the person demands an interior wholeness. Adolescents and adults need to integrate mind and heart, lest the sense of person, of *who I am*, becomes profoundly threatened.

Religion deals with the supernatural, of course, and cannot be encompassed totally by our rational concepts, yet the Christian Faith is completely reasonable and rational. In meditation, the reasoning mind is put into communication, so to speak, with the truths of the Faith. Truth is like light to the reasoning mind, which is made to desire this light, and to recognize it as beautiful and right when it presents itself. In adolescence this desire for truth, and sensitivity to truth and to falsity, is radically increased in the person beyond what it was in the child. For this reason, it is in adolescence that meditation should be first encountered and practiced. Many adults, who have well-developed and educated intellects, have never learned to practice meditation in a formal sense. Fortunately God is patient with us! A gray-haired man or woman seeking to grow in prayer, even returning to learn what may be most basic, is a beautiful witness to the grace and the love of God.

Beginning strongly in adolescence, and continuing into adulthood, the human mind is made increasingly to desire truth. We need to integrate this growing capacity and desire for truth into our prayer. If we did not learn meditation in our sensitive adolescent years, this lack of knowledge will have serious consequences in our experience of prayer as adults. We will find, in the crises and challenges of adult life, that we have intellectually outgrown the vocal prayers of our childhood. The old formula prayers will not seem satisfying or appropriate. Vocal prayer as we knew it as children will no longer be sufficient to our adolescent or adult needs, and we begin to experience an interior schism. This is a most dangerous spiritual challenge, and a time of great danger to the soul. The adolescent needs prayer appropriate to his growing mind and will; the adult needs prayer appropriate to the adult experience. The needs of the maturing personal soul for appropriate, authentic, rational communication with God in prayer can not be ignored without most serious spiritual consequence.

When appropriate prayer life is ignored, a huge gulf develops and continues growing into adulthood — a gulf between the genuine need for relationship with God and the personal means of entering that relationship. Prayer is our communication with God, and communication is absolutely essential to relationship. Many disaffected and alienated adults today, even in the Church, are in this serious condition because they did not grow in prayer as they grew emotionally and intellectually. The appropriate methodological tool needed for intellectual communication and intellectual relationship with God is meditation.

Discursive meditation is defined as the application of reason to some spiritual truth in order to engage its meaning, to penetrate its meaning, and to integrate the truth into one's life. Mental activity and attention are clearly required, and the first goal is the enlightenment of the mind with the truth. It is important to realize that Christian meditation is not achieved with the simple presence in the mind of some truth; the ultimate goal is the integration of that truth into one's life.

The final goal of meditation, then, is personal transformation of one's life, to life in Christ. Meditation calls forth change in the way we live. Several intermediate stages in meditation present themselves. First, the mind is enlightened with some truth, for the purpose (in the intellect) of forming firm convictions, of forming intellectual consent to this truth. This conviction, and consent to the truth, is itself for the purpose of arousing the right response within the will to truth: this right response is love. This is the most important of the interior results of meditation, the arousal of love because of supernatural truth. Yet the purpose of prayer is not finally this interior affection only, but truth needs to be expressed by the whole person. That is, the final goal of meditation is a life of active charity in Christ.

Adolescents are action-oriented, and many adults also are impatient with any suggestion of sitting and thinking for its own sake. It is important to realize that the final goal of meditation is not to "sit and meditate," so to speak: it is Christian action. Our thoughts about meditation have been influenced and even confused by Eastern mystics and gurus. Christian meditation does not seek trances and introspection, but divine light and fire for Christian living. Our purpose in meditation is zeal, and the virtuous action of a life in Christ.

There are several schools of meditation, each with specific methods.[2] The general structures of the various methods have in common three essential parts: first, the engagement of one's thought with some supernatural truth, second, the examination of one's life in the light of that truth, and finally the conviction for action, to enact that truth with one's life. This basic pattern is essentially practical and reasonable to any of us, both adolescents and adults.

The most helpful truths to be approached in meditation are age-specific and person-specific. In the matter of what is to be meditated upon, one's age, religious background and experiences, and education all become relevant. Fortunately, the selection of themes helpful for you or for me in meditation is not a major problem. Examples of themes suitable to meditation and relevant to the person of whatever age abound in Scripture and other sources in the Church. The goal is life in Christ, and the deeper and truer relationship with Him that supernaturally produces holiness of life. As we become more and more alert to the work of the Holy Spirit in our lives, we will begin to notice the many ways He directs us to particular passages of Scripture, and to particular themes and truths of God. He guides and moves us in our real needs, to the real and corresponding truths which can heal us and draw us even more fully to our goal.

Praying Scripture

There is much that could be said about the many ways one might approach Scripture prayerfully. Before we discuss a method, however, we must discuss attitude.

1. We do not *use* Scripture as we would pick up and use some tool. Scripture must be approached with the reverence due it as the Word of God. It is not for us to use, but to hear. In order to hear, we must listen, with attention and devotion.

2. We do not listen to Scripture in order to gain information, but to gain formation. That is, in God is the truth that can form us rightly, and bring order and peace to a life that is confused and incomplete. We are not gathering data, but seeking the beautiful and healing wisdom of God.

3. We do not look in Scripture for saints or even for Jesus in order to merely admire them or pay them due respect. God had an intention, a purpose, in creating you and me. Our fulfillment requires the personal wholehearted engagement of our selves with the divine and eternal truth of God. We look in Scripture, with ready response, for our vocation. "Jesus, what do You want me to *do*?"

Pray - Study - Pray

One method for praying Scripture is found in the formula "pray - study - pray." This method seeks to avoid the various partial and wrong approaches to Scripture, and to instead present ourselves to God in His Word as we reverently listen. To force ourselves to a balance of both attention and devotion, we set aside equal total times. If I allow 15 minutes of initial prayer of the passage, then I set aside 30 minutes of study and 15 minutes again of prayer of the passage. If I can give 10 minutes of initial prayer to the passage, then I set aside 20 minutes for study of the passage followed by 10 minutes again of prayer. In this way study and prayer are balanced at least outwardly, and I am attempting to listen with both mind and heart.[3]

In the sequence of "pray - study - pray" we want to cooperate with the requirements of meditation. Our hope is to apply our minds, our reason, to some spiritual truth we find in Scripture in order personally to engage and penetrate its meaning, and then to integrate that truth into our life. In our initial prayer, then, we read the passage slowly and carefully, seeking to be present to the Word and to allow the Word to be present to us. We want to listen without prejudice, without presupposition, without any intention to bend the Word to our own understanding. We listen, in other words, to the witness of *another person*, to testimony we do not yet possess. We listen in genuine personal openness.

In the time allotted to study, we seek to uncover the truth in the Word, and understand it, gathering it into our own storehouse of knowledge. Here we become students of Scripture, following references to other passages, reading commentaries by trustworthy scholars, searching into the meanings of particular words, and so on. We seek the truth witnessed to in the Scripture, as light for the intellects God gave us.

In the final time of prayer, then, we are ready to receive what God has revealed to us. Having really engaged our minds with some supernatural truth, we are ready to examine our life in the light of that truth, and make resolutions for action. The meditation prepares us to enact, to incarnate, that truth in our life. These truths do not have to be precepts, or rules of life. Truth is revealed fully in the life of Christ, and this life can declare imperatives for us in many ways. The key is to listen with openness, with an obedient heart.

Lectio Divina

Deep within the monastic spirituality of the Church is the prayer of "holy reading" of Scripture, lectio divina.[4] This is a traditional method of meditation of Scripture, comprised of the four stages lectio, meditatio, oratio, and contemplatio. In lectio, the sacred text is read slowly and even audibly, allowing the Word to be heard interiorly and exteriorly, so to speak. After the time of reading, in meditatio, the soul takes time to ponder the Word heard. Here the Bread of the Word can be chewed thoroughly, and swallowed. Next, in oratio, our response in spoken prayer to God begins. Having heard, having pondered and understood His Word to *me* as a person, I have a response: perhaps a plea for true faith or deeper understanding, perhaps a cry of fear or a call for strength, perhaps a song of happy praise and thanksgiving. Last is the stage of contemplatio that is a time of quiet resting with Him and in Him. We have communicated: we have heard our God, considered His Word carefully, responded to Him from both mind and heart, and now we sit quietly with Him in silent and loving adoration.

Affective Prayer: Warming the Heart

After meditation, which we have been considering, comes affective prayer, the next stage after meditation in the development of ascetical prayer. It is a natural progression, in a sense, from successful meditation. It is a movement of emphasis in prayer, more than a distinct stage in itself. The emphasis in meditation is upon enlightenment in the mind; the emphasis in affective prayer is in the will, with the virtue of charity.

The arousal of divine love is of course a goal in meditation. Even before meditation, the beginning seeds of love are found in effective vocal prayer, in its requirement of heartfelt devotion. But in this stage we consider now, affective prayer, the prayer communication with God has become simpler, less verbal, less symbolic, more immediate. Here the prayer is moving the human person into a closer stage of intimacy, closer to the heart of our Lord.

As was the case with meditation, affective prayer is a needed and appropriate way of communicating with God, which becomes particularly appropriate in the adolescent years and continues through adulthood. As with meditation, Christians who do not grow into this way of praying into their adult prayer life will become restricted in their relationship with God. An emerging part of their human personality, their affective dimension, will not find connection with absolute truth. The heart-to-heart bridge to God will be equivocal and uncertain, resulting in a serious alienation within the soul, for a person with this kind of retarded prayer development.

Affective prayer is centered mainly in the will, and as such is experienced with emotion. The presence of emotion alone while praying is not a sure indicator of affective prayer, however. A person can experience powerful emotion while praying, yet emotion resulting from something other than communion with God. The object of true affective prayer is God, and communion with Him in the virtue of charity. This is a communion in love with God which is accompanied with the authentic emotions of love. Lesser loves can also bring emotion, even powerful if unfocused emotion.

Some adults are especially prone, by nature, to emotional expression. Many adolescents, because of the emotional growth taking place in them at this time, experience unstable and unpredictable centers of emotion within themselves. For such people emotional expression is unpredictable and unreliable in its meaning. The experience of emotion itself, even in the context of prayer, cannot guarantee the deeper stage of prayer relationship with God that we seek, affective prayer. This is plainly true even in the analogous case of human relationships: strong feelings of attraction between teens, or even between adults, cannot guarantee the presence of authentic, enduring and self-giving love.

Some religious services, such as revivals and prayer meetings, may be very emotional by design and intention. This can be spiritually dangerous and misleading to an undiscerning person who attends such a service, exactly as persons can be misled by emotion in their interpersonal relationships. Two persons can feel powerful surges of emotion toward each other, which seem to be from the depths of their hearts, and yet have no real basis for covenantal love. In the same way, some religious leaders can be skilled at drawing forth powerful surges of emotion from their audience, yet fail to enable the kind of real contact with God that is covenantal and transforming.

At the other extreme are those persons who have difficulty allowing and expressing emotion itself. Some adults who did not successfully integrate the emerging dimension of emotion in their adolescent years, can remain stunted in that area in all their later relationships. Hence in their prayer life, the real experience of heartfelt love for the God they seek is very difficult. These people may find meditation natural and easy, at least in an outward sense. They may find the intellectual encounter with God in prayer easy, but are blocked in further development. This is as serious a problem, in prayer development, as is the other extreme.

The solution to the problem of growing in prayer, for a person having difficulty with emotions at one extreme or the other, may be as simple as paying attention to the road. That is, the road to deeper prayer begins at the beginning, and progresses through stages. Authentic affective prayer is enabled through authentic meditation, which is entered after effective vocal prayer. Affective prayer can be considered even as less a separate stage of prayer than a fulfillment of meditation: the two are linked both in theory and in practice. In other words, we need to grow into a full emotional experience of prayer but only based on the right foundation.

The human heart was made to respond fully, humanly, emotionally, authentically, to *truth*. The mind was made to recognize truth, and to present it, so to speak, to the heart for loving acceptance. The mind was made to recognize it; the heart, to respond to it. If our emotions are ungrounded in truth, they are still powerful, but they are unreliable as guides. The beautiful feelings of affective prayer, the feelings of love, come forth naturally as a completing of what has begun in the soul in meditation.

Entering Affective Prayer

Affective prayer is safely entered and experienced through the door of meditation. When you are meditating, for example with some passage in Scripture, you will discover feelings naturally aroused in the presence of divine truth. The will is made to respond to truth, and it does. The brighter and clearer is the truth grasped in the mind, the more beautiful and desirable is it to the will. In this way meditation enlightens the mind, and naturally begins to enkindle the will. The heart responds with love to the beauty of truth, and the will is moved to enact it personally.

In the prayer of meditation, pondering and studying some passage of Scripture for example, the heart will at times and to differing degrees be moved with feelings. When this happens, you should not try to force the heart one way or the other. You should not try to amplify these feelings, nor to stifle them. If you are disciplining yourself with a method of meditation, for example the "pray - study - pray" sequence of the last section, you should set the method aside and let your heart respond. God is allowing you to experience the beginnings of a deeper prayer, and you must allow yourself to experience it as well. If you are trying to "study," but find yourself moved to love and worship, allow this movement to happen. When the feelings subside, then is the time to simply continue in the meditation you had begun. Meditation will naturally lead to these experiences, and we must allow the growth to happen.

Vocal prayer, both spontaneous and formula, will be refined, purified and deepened with growth in meditation and in affective prayer. Progress in prayer does not mean the abandonment of these more basic ways of prayer, vocal prayer, but rather their enrichment.

Importance of the First Stages

We need to learn and experience affective prayer, then, but only as the natural progression from meditation. The spiritual development of the soul calls for both enlightenment of the mind through meditation and formation of the heart in charity through affective prayer. A person who has not learned to engage his mind rightly in prayer, through meditation, may be wounded in further development in several ways. Not only may he be disabled in further growth into affective prayer, but he also may begin to experience the lethal intellectual dualism of this age. He may begin to believe in a separation between his reason and his religious life, precisely because his mind and his heart have not found unity in divine truth. Soon the wrong thinking of this age can begin to seem right to him: religion is irrational, it is a fantasy. His religious life may then be placed in a box by itself, isolated from both mind and heart. His religion as a consequence then becomes isolated from all reality, to be abandoned or discounted.

Affective prayer, based on the engagement of the mind with the mind of Christ, engages the heart with the heart of Christ. It enables communication with His charity, and therefore brings forth the fruit of the works of His charity. A life of increasing virtue, along with the subjective feelings of love, are marks of affective prayer. The call to follow Christ is an objective call: it is a call to incarnate divine truth. This is a vocation to true heroism, requiring more of the soul than mere mental ascent, more also than mere feelings. A heart-bond is needed in truth, to walk after Jesus in the hard times. There will be suffering in the Christian life. There will be struggles, and spiritual battles. A union deeper than that gained in the beauty of His truth is necessary, yet it must be based upon that truth. The union of minds, and the even more interior union of wills is imperative, in the bond of divine charity. This union of wills and of hearts is sought in the communication of affective prayer. The bond of this prayer has the strength to carry a cross behind the Lord, because it is the bond of love.

It is important again to emphasize that we never outgrow our need for vocal prayer, although we do outgrow the conversations of childhood. Vocal prayer, in the more mature years that begin in adolescence, needs the depth and dimension enabled by both meditation and affective prayer. Without the intellectual depth formed in meditation, vocal prayer can seem childish and irrational to the adolescent and the adult. Without the depth of heart, of emotion, of conviction in the will formed in affective prayer, vocal prayer can seem hypocritical and irrelevant. Such vocal prayer will indeed be irrelevant to worldly and materialistic heart-desires that dominate the secular culture around us.

Unanswered needs in adolescence can become crippling infirmities in adulthood. The way of God is to integrate all the emerging faculties of the person, as he grows into the Truth. The mind needs the communication with Truth which meditation enables; the will needs the formation and foundation in the heart-intentions of God which are enabled in affective prayer. The adult who has not grown with proper prayer formation may be seriously restricted in his ability to communicate with God, and this may have most serious consequences for his whole actualization as a person. We need to learn to pray with the wholeness of our human personality. If we would be present with God, we must present ourselves wholly to Him. Vocal prayer leads naturally, then, into meditation which is completed with affective prayer.

Prayer of Simplicity

This stage of prayer is more difficult in a sense to characterize, because of its simplicity. It is a resting before God with an enlightened mind and a quiet heart. This is the highest form of ascetical prayer, in the sense that it is close, outwardly speaking, to the beginnings of mystical prayer through infused contemplation. This prayer of simplicity, however, is ascetical prayer; this is prayer accessible to the person by his own effort, through ordinary grace. The ordinary path to this prayer is through meditation that enlightens the mind with the transforming truths of God, and through affective prayer that draws the will into union with the will of God.

This prayer is easily misunderstood because of its outward appearance of simplicity. A person who is not inwardly simple might look upon outward simplicity with condescension if not scorn. Someone approaching the prayer of simplicity prematurely, who has not been rightly formed beforehand into simplicity toward God, might try to imitate simplicity in outward methodologies while inwardly remaining in complexity and confusion. Right formation in the mind and heart is necessary to enter this prayer, which consists more of rest than of any activity. It should be clear, however, that it is not wise to try to force oneself, or anyone else, into this prayer. The prayer of simplicity is a way of prayer which "suggests itself" to the soul ready for it. In fact, of course, it is the Lord Himself who works this growth into deeper prayer. Thought becomes simpler and quiet in meditation, and the will calmer in affective prayer, as the soul moves (so to speak) more closely to the Lord in the prayer of simplicity.

The prayer of simplicity is in a sense an "advanced" form of prayer. It may be sadly true that many Christians do not attain this place of peace before the Lord in prayer, but this prayer is within the reach of adolescents, and should be normal to adults. As was asserted about the stages of meditation and affective prayer, it is also asserted here that a real human need for the prayer of simplicity begins in adolescence and continues into adulthood.

We all have need of peace and quiet, becoming more aware of the need as we get older. The particular need for inner calm, beginning in adolescence, is amplified by the pervading opposite — the almost ever-present *noise* — in much of contemporary society. The society we live in sadly offers little toward the wholeness, peace and interior integration of persons. Much secular culture today is antagonistic to peace, instead feeding inner conflict and disharmony. The interior life is commonly assaulted in our culture by chaotic and rebellious music, by violent, sensuous movies and television, and by insulting and demeaning fictional caricatures of human life. Leaders in our culture often promote education of the mind for only mercenary purposes, and dedication of the will to mere self-gratification. The authentic human desires for self-giving, for committed love, for interior peace and wholeness are often ignored.

We should not be surprised when young persons formed in such a dehumanized environment then are tempted to drown themselves in a cacophony of noise — audible, visual, and tactile. Persons who come into physical adulthood deprived of fully human formation can hardly be expected to have the emotional, intellectual, or spiritual maturity they need and deserve. Human persons need quiet, peace, and an interior life.

The prayer of simplicity is a resting before God, a quiet and peaceful waiting in His presence. This is a possibility for a soul having found enlightenment of mind and integrity of heart in Christ. Adolescents and adults are naturally ready for the relationship with God that enables such enlightenment and integrity, through meditation and affective prayer. In adulthood, we need the fullness of these stages of prayer. The person who has been rightly formed by such praying will be led more and more to simpler prayer, moving finally into the quiet resting presence with God that is described here as "the prayer of simplicity."

The fruit of such prayer is a calm, and a personal integrity, which is a crown of righteousness for a person of any age.

Entering the Prayer of Simplicity

As was true of the stages preceding it, this prayer suggests itself to the soul ready for it. Again to use the example of a person who has chosen the method of "pray - study - pray" to listen to Scripture, and has moved through meditation into affective prayer, the prayer of simplicity begins in the soul very naturally. First, meditation exposes the soul to true and absolute beauty: the self-revelation of God in His Word. The will is moved to enact this truth, to express it (to express God) in human living. The heart responds with deep affection, with feelings of profound love for God the Source of all truth. Hence a human life is moved to renewal and conversion, to live a more faithful Christian life. Hence also the soul is deeply warmed within. The soul experiences love interiorly as the person manifests exteriorly a more faithful walk with Christ. These true feelings of love, so enkindled, invite the soul into an intimate and interior rest with the Lord who has so revealed Himself. This quiet and peaceful resting is called the prayer of simplicity, and is the most intimate communication with God we have yet discussed. This is the epitome of ascetical prayer, but far more is still awaiting the soul in mystical prayer.

The prayer of simplicity is entered through invitation, so to speak, experienced in the heart-relationship felt in affective prayer. As you allow your heart to experience the loving movements stirred by truth in meditation, setting aside the discipline of "pray - study - pray" for example, these loving movements will themselves grow simpler in time. As affective prayer becomes more and more an ordinary prayer experience for you, the soul will want and need less and less assurance by the mind, so to speak, of the truth set before it. Less mental reflection will be required, and the heart will more easily be moved to joy in the truth of the Lord. The soul will gladly be quiet, will wait in peace, and simply rest at His feet. You must then cooperate with the developing relationship in your soul with the Lord, and allow the moment of quiet rest to be, and as it suggests itself, to become.

Conclusions Regarding Ascetical Prayer

Many Catholic adults have little formal knowledge of prayer beyond the formula prayers they learned in childhood. This is not to say that such Catholics necessarily pray poorly or inadequately. But if such Catholics experience difficulty praying with a sense of real communication with God, it may well be because their prayer has never advanced beyond childhood. The beautiful formula prayers we learn in our youth are lacking nothing in themselves, but if as adults we pray them with no more depth than that learned as children, then our prayer as communication is lacking. Without doubt some adults have experienced great depths in prayer with no formal teachings on it, but these generous blessings of God do not excuse our obligation before God to actively seek Him, to do all that is in our power to grow toward Him.

The Church has a great treasure of spiritual theology, with wonderful and profound understandings of the interior life of prayer. These understandings must be part of real Christian lives of real human persons, however, or it is all academic. As Catholics we need a personal relationship with God in prayer, and we deserve to benefit from the wisdom of the Church. Beginning in adolescence, and becoming more urgent as adult years pass, we need to grow in prayer relationship with God. The stages of ascetical prayer, which we can grow through with the ordinary graces of the Christian life, mark our ordinary journey to holiness.

GROWTH IN THE PURGATIVE STAGE

The Mansions of St. Teresa

St. Teresa of Avila pictures the human soul as a castle, more beautiful than we can imagine because it was created in the very image and likeness of His Majesty, our Lord.[5] It is in entering this castle that one enters the spiritual life, entering really *oneself*, the interior life of the soul. The castle then is further pictured as having many mansions or dwelling places, which are numbered as one moves more and more to the interior.

The initial entrance into the castle, into the first mansion, is made by the door of prayer and reflection. In the beginnings of real prayer there must be reflection, Teresa insists, at least some of the time. She recognizes that in the beginning a person will be frequently distracted and preoccupied with the things of the world, but without at least some reflection upon the majesty of God who is addressed in beginning vocal prayer, Teresa doubts that authentic prayer is occurring. She writes, "A prayer in which a person is not aware of whom he is speaking to, what he is asking, who it is who is asking and of whom, I do not call prayer however much the lips move."[6]

If a beginner in prayer were to pick up Teresa's *Interior Castle* in order to learn how to pray, the person might be disappointed. Her work is not a "how to do it" kind of book, but she does describe much about prayer that is essential to know. For example, as Teresa writes of the journey through the first three mansions, she writes little specifically about prayer as such, but much more of the sins and temptations which assail the soul in living. The struggles of the beginner to actually and earnestly begin, are critical. One must turn away from sin and begin the journey toward God.

There is not complete unanimity among spiritual writers on harmonizing the stages of ascetical prayer, as we have described them, with the first few interior mansions as St. Teresa saw and described them. Nor is there full agreement on correlating her complete seven mansions with the traditionally accepted three stages of the spiritual life: beginner, proficient, perfect. It is important to know that the differences among scholars are not significant, however, and the general movement of the soul's progression to spiritual perfection in Christ is clear in the slightly differing frameworks. St. Teresa's work in spiritual theology is of enormous importance, and certainly cannot be ignored or neglected, even given slight differences of opinion in exactly how to incorporate her seven mansions into the overall theology. One framework is offered in Table 1 below, which illustrates the movement in the person in both prayer and life, so to speak, as he cooperates with the Holy Spirit drawing him through the purgative stage to God.

Table 1 outlines a way to correlate Teresa's initial three interior mansions with the growth of prayer in the purgative stage. God may well allow other paths, other correspondences! What seems to be normative, however, is the correspondence of progress in one's prayer life with one's moral life. Prayer reflects our intimacy with God, which demands our faithfulness to Him.

Mystical Prayer: The Radical Event of Contemplation

Table 1: Prayer in the Purgative Stage, the Stage of the Beginners	
Stages of Prayer	**The Seven Mansions of St. Teresa**
Initially: *Vocal Prayer* with usual dependence on *Formula Prayers*	*First Mansions:* The new relationship with Christ is tenuous, and half-hearted. Still strongly attracted to worldly matters and pleasures, still respectful of honors and ambitions, the person must work to overcome temptation. He becomes generally free from intentional serious sin, but the world has a dangerous attraction. The person must turn away from sin, putting aside unnecessary worldly affairs, and must intentionally focus upon the things of God and His kingdom.
Vocal prayer includes more spontaneity; formula prayers become more meaningful. *Meditation* begins to enlighten the mind, leading into *Affective Prayer* which en-kindles a will for the things of God.	*Second Mansions:* Worldly pastimes are partially renounced but partially kept. He hears the call of the Lord, but remains weak and divided. The soul is torn between two loves, between the world and the eternal. He vacillates between wanting to return to the first mansions, and to persevere and go on. He is still a child in the virtues of humility, obedience, love, and patience. He should avoid mixing with mediocre or evil people, and should rather seek out the good and the more mature. The need is to persevere, and to embrace the Cross.
Prayer becomes increasingly simple, less verbal, more a quiet rest with God. The *Prayer of Simplicity*.	*Third Mansions:* The person here has persevered and his conscience has become more sensitive. He increasingly is careful not to offend God, avoiding even venial sins. He has overcome much temptation, and has begun to embrace the cross with Christ. Penance and recollection become goods to embrace. He uses time well, practices charity, is careful in speech and dress. The need remains to be attentive; to walk carefully in fear and humility.

When St. Teresa begins to describe the fourth of the seven mansions of the soul, she entrusts herself even more especially to the Holy Spirit, and asks for His aid. These fourth mansions are especially difficult to discuss and important to explain, because "supernatural experiences begin here."[7] Grades of prayer prior to this are called ascetical, and as we have observed are possible for us to do with ordinary grace. Beginning with infused contemplation, however, God becomes the active one. We can at most be faithful cooperators with the work of communication which God alone can do in the soul.

It is here in the fourth mansions that mystical prayer begins, and here God directly, immediately, begins His work in the soul of a human person for spiritual transformation. It is here that the mystical life begins, with entrance into the illuminative stage of the spiritual journey. It is here that the person leaves the stage of beginners, and enters the stage of the proficients. There is no guarantee that the transition is permanent, or that the growth is complete, because we can fall back! A person who falls back is in spiritual danger, but he can begin again. It is possible, however, that a soul can fall back and never again receive the graces God may be offering him. But in this new stage of spiritual communication with God, a radically new and different relationship exists and is offered to the soul. God now begins to do what He only can do, a work which we most desperately need, in order to make our way into His loving heart.

Although God is primarily the active one in this very important stage of prayer, the person is not completely passive. He must prepare for it most importantly with desire, striving to do all he knows to do to turn against all sin and away from the fleeting treasures of this transient world. And he must strive to seek God, to go to God, to be with the Lord. When the Lord then desires to grace this soul with His presence, the person must hold on to the graces he is given; he must remain faithful to all he receives. This is not easy, because grace is multiplying in him, and more and more is now possible to him. "Every one to whom much is given, of him will much be required" (Lk 12:48).

Transition to Mystical Prayer: The Dark Night of the Senses

The person advancing into deeper prayer relationship with God begins to experience, at the entrance to the mystical life, a necessary but troubling and even painful purgation called a "dark night". Defects exist in the beginner, in spite of his zeal to be faithful, which can be corrected only by the sovereign hand of God. Fr. Garrigou-Lagrange writes that the spiritual defects may be reduced to three: spiritual pride, spiritual sensuality, and spiritual sloth.[8]

The person can become too attached to those blessings, those "sensible consolations" that God sometimes gives for encouragement to beginners in prayer. The person can become too fond of the wonderful feelings aroused by the love and acceptance and forgiveness of God that he has experienced. This is understandable, but the soul needs to learn to love God for Himself, not merely for what He can do for us. The soul must learn to seek not its own pleasure in the blessings of God, but rather God as He is in Himself. Therefore *spiritual sensuality*, sometimes called spiritual gluttony, must be purged from the soul. This requires the withdrawal on God's part of these sensual experiences from the person: hence a time of sensual aridity, and darkness.

Spiritual sloth, which is an impatience or even disgust toward spiritual effort, can then reveal itself within the soul when the consolations it was accustomed to are withdrawn. How dangerous this dark night can be for the soul! How humiliating these tendencies within us! Yet this is so far a temptation, not a sin, if the soul does not succumb. Also called acedia, the spiritual disgust can lead the person to evil intent, to rancor, to negativity, to discouragement and to cowardice.

Spiritual pride, on the other hand, arises when God does not withdraw the outward blessings and consolations from the soul. The person then thinks more highly of himself than he should, and he assumes himself worthy and deserving of God's blessings and graces. Such a person then considers himself a master of spiritual matters and a teacher of others, when he is only a child and a beginner!

These basic and fundamental defects within the soul in even earnest beginners require a work from the outside, so to speak. There is much that a person can do to purge himself of sin, and he needs to do all that he can do, but there are limits. In the dark night of the senses, God Himself does for the soul what it cannot do for itself, to continue the proper reformation of the person, the interior reordering. The senses must be brought under submission to the spirit, and the spirit to God, for the soul to be at peace. Thus the passive purification of the senses, in the first dark night, is necessary.

St. John of the Cross describes three crucial signs in the person of the arrival of the dark night of the senses.[9] They are summarized in Table 2, following a similar one given by Fr. Garrigou-Lagrange.[10]

The presence of all three signs, all present together in a person, is confirmation of God's work and this dark night having begun. These signs must be present, this night must come, prior to God's gift of Himself in infused contemplation, and advanced stages of prayer. With a keen desire to serve God, the soul fears that it does not, and is instead sharply aware of its sins and weaknesses. This fear is the fear of a son who loves his father, not the servile fear of a slave fearing punishment. The soul truly wants to serve God because of the worthiness of God, yet despairs because of its own unworthiness. God does not grant the soul the pleasant feelings of before, nor give the material blessings and protections. God is becoming more present to the soul than ever, but the soul, looking for God in the ways of the past, is not able to perceive Him. God is awaiting now more interiorly, so to speak, and the soul must find Him anew in this more interior place. Hence the soul experiences darkness, aloneness, and suffering, even though God is more authentically and really active and present than ever before. There is great need then for perseverance, enduring in faith in Him beyond anything that can be felt, seen, or understood. Faithful endurance is the active response of the soul; the person must actively choose to passively receive the work that only God can accomplish.

Table 2: Signs of the Dark Night of the Senses	
Psychological Experiences	**Theological Explanation**
1. One finds no consolation in the things of God, nor in created things.	Activity of the gift of knowledge, showing the emptiness of created things and the gravity of sin.
2. One keenly desires to serve God, with a thirst for justice and fear of sin. One finds strength in time of temptation.	Activity of the gift of fortitude, with the gift of fear.
3. There is great difficulty in discursive meditation, with instead a tendency to the simple affective gaze toward God.	Activity of the gift of understanding; the beginning of infused contemplation.

The Prayer of Quiet: St. Teresa's Fourth Mansions

In the fourth mansions of the soul Teresa describes the prayer of quiet. This prayer experience brings a great release to the soul, a great and new freedom. The soul loses the former constraints in its service to God that it had because of fear — servile fear — connected fundamentally with the fear of hell. There is now an even greater fear of offending God than before, but now because of Who He is, and His holiness. Before, there was much fear of any suffering, hardships or penances which might be required in the spiritual journey, but now great confidence replaces that fear. Faith is now more alive, and trials and suffering are viewed with courage and with hope in God. The increased sense of the glory of God results in an increased sense of the person's own unworthiness, and gives the person a clear view that the world's delights are as mere rubble compared to the things of God.

Teresa gives a strong warning to anyone in this state, of the very serious need of perseverance. "In this prayer the soul is not yet grown but is like a suckling child. If it turns away from its mother's breasts, what can be expected for it but death?"[11] We must take notice: withdrawal from God's grace is entirely possible to a person here. The individual will be greatly tempted and tried by the Devil, since that evil spirit knows the great goods that are possible for the kingdom of God through such a graced soul. Spiritual combat with satanic forces should be expected, because the evil one will not let God's kingdom gain without a struggle. The Devil will try to counterfeit God's graces, and will tempt the soul toward pride and vainglory. True humility, and steadfast perseverance are needed here.

The Prayer of Union: St. Teresa's Fifth Mansions

St. Teresa associates this prayer with an experience of the soul with God, an experience with several unique characteristics. The person knows he is not asleep, but neither does he seem to be awake. The faculties of his soul are indeed asleep — unresponsive — to the things of this world and even to himself. The person doesn't have the power even to think as he wants to. The experience seems to be death in a sense, yet a "delightful one", an entering of the soul more perfectly in God.[12] The reasoning intellect wants to understand what is being felt, yet has no energy to do this.

During this unusual prayer of union the person doubts the experience itself, and he wonders if perhaps it is all imagination and not true communication with God. Perhaps he is asleep, or perhaps the Devil is deceiving him. The person has many suspicions, but Teresa assures us that in the true prayer of union the Devil can have no access into the soul, nor can he do any harm. True union occurs in the interior of the soul, a place the Devil cannot enter. Other "unions" so to speak exist, which the Devil can use for his purposes, but not this which is purely spiritual. Lesser earthly experiences of pleasure, joy, and satisfaction can be used by the Devil. Teresa explains that these unions differ, as feelings on the outer surface of the body differ from those in the marrow of the bones.[13] This prayer of union is deeply interior, and completely spiritual, and is one of profound delight and joy.

Uncertainty exists nevertheless during the prayer experience, which is brief, yet afterwards when the soul returns to itself, it has the certitude that this was indeed God. Even years afterward, there can be no doubt that the soul was in God, and God was in the soul.[14] Teresa explains that this confidence comes out of such an uncertain experience not because of seeing or touching something, but because God places confidence in the soul.

The results of this prayer of union prove the reality of it, for it is a union of the will of the person with the will of God. His will is for our love, as in the two great commandments of love of God and love of neighbor. The fundamental result of the prayer within the person is then union with the will of God to love. This gain of great love leads further to the gain of freedom with regard to suffering. Rather than being inhibited or even crippled in the Christian expression of God's love, because of fear of suffering, the person is instead free simply to love. Even great suffering can now be heroically endured for the sake of God's love.

There begins through this prayer a personal identification with the suffering love of Christ, who counted suffering as nothing in comparison with His love for souls, and His desire to save us. Teresa writes, "Oh great delight, to suffer in doing the will of God!"[15] There is in fact great interior suffering because of the keen realization of our failures to love as we ought. In a painfully clear light of the realization of the love of God, there is intense infused grief over sin in the world, and one's own inability to serve God well enough.

This supernatural union with His will also means that the soul gains His desire, now becoming strong in the person, for the person's own perfection. The close relationship between suffering and the perfection of the soul is now perceived in the light of God. Suffering is seen as necessary to this perfection, and any cost is acceptable and well worth it. We do not lose our humanity, or our ability to experience suffering in times of loss, trials, or sickness. But in this stage of union we accept such sufferings as in His perfect will, and our will is at peace in His.

In this stage of prayer we are not infallible, nor is it impossible to fall. Teresa warns us of the dangers of this stage, that we might keep close watch on the way we are walking in it. The will of God is clear: to love Him completely, and to love our neighbor as ourselves. We can deceive ourselves easily about our love for God. Our real and actual love of neighbor is the test to keep before our eyes. She writes, "If we fail in love of neighbor we are lost."[16] We need to be alert to any tendency to become complacent, or presumptuous. We must rather strive always to move forward in the way of holiness and love, forcing if necessary our will to submit to the will of others, to seek their welfare above our own alone even if we lose our rights in the process. It will cost us to participate in the loving self-giving of God! It will cost us to take up our own cross to follow Jesus.

Satan also is not inactive in this stage, but tries to deceive the soul under the guise of good. He tries to cause confusion in any small matter, to create darkness in the intellect and cooling in the will. He seeks to cause an increase in self-love, to draw the soul away from the saving will of God. Again, perseverance and endurance is needed. We must continue in prayer, seeking God's loving sustenance.

In trying to explain this stage of prayer and spiritual intimacy with God, Teresa uses the analogy of human love in sacramental marriage. This stage of the union is only the first level in the final three mansions of St. Teresa, which together bring the fullness of the intention of God in the person. Teresa likens this prayer to the meeting of the man and the woman before the betrothal for marriage. It is like "the joining of hands"; it is a sharing and a commitment, but not complete or final.

Teresa's analogy fits our understanding of sacramental marriage if we envision the soul as feminine, the woman in the wedding, appropriate to the Bridegroom who is Christ. In this way we see that we, as the Church who is the Bride of Christ (Rv 21), are in a sense all "woman" to Him. It is therefore appropriate to refer to the soul as feminine, as Teresa in fact does.

The soul then expresses this stage of relationship with her beloved, and becomes "well informed about the goodness of her Spouse and determined to do His will in everything and in as many ways as she sees will make Him happy."[17] This likening to a relationship moving toward marriage is of course intentional, for He is in fact the intended Bridegroom of the soul. This analogy will continue into the final stages of the spiritual journey to our destiny, and the final perfection of charity in Him.

The Prayer of Conforming Union: St. Teresa's Sixth Mansions, The Dark Night of the Spirit

In the sixth mansions, the soul enters the stage of prayer communication called conforming union, and experiences spiritual betrothal with the divine Bridegroom. This is not mere poetic language, it describes a real spiritual union with God. The relationship is signified in analogy with that of engagement between human persons prior to their marriage. The soul deeply desires oneness with God, and is resolved to seek no other, but to be joined together with Him forever. The divine Bridegroom, however, sees that even stronger desire is needed, and a cost must be paid. Teresa calls this betrothal "the greatest of blessings", requiring interior and exterior trials yet to be suffered.[18] The effect of this prayer in the person is the conforming of desire in the soul to the desire of the Bridegroom. The holiness and intimacy of this union is obviously both deep and profound.

Teresa describes many misunderstandings that a soul in

this trial will experience. Others will accuse the person of merely pretending sanctity, of seeking praise from others, of outward show or even of being deceived by Satan. The few who speak well of the person are an even greater trial within the person, because he sees clearly to the contrary his own unworthiness and poverty. God may send the person at this time severe illness, and acute pain. Teresa remarked that the pains were so intense for her that she would gladly have suffered martyrdom, rather than continue with them, although they came in brief intervals.[19] Other torments come from those the person looks to for help: one's confessor, or spiritual advisor. The only real help for the person, Teresa counsels, is from God in His mercy. The person must endure the trial with faith: "This severe suffering comes so that one may enter the seventh dwelling place."[20]

The extreme trial and suffering that Teresa describes in her sixth mansions correlate with what St. John of the Cross calls the dark night of the spirit. This is the final and severe purgation of the soul, to prepare it for full union with God. This passive purgation and dark night, in the theological structure of the spiritual life given by St. John of the Cross, is the necessary entrance to the unitive way, the way of the perfect. Entrance to the illuminative way from the purgative way was necessarily through a dark night of the senses, which St. Peter and the apostles experienced in the trials of the passion. The enlightenment of a beginner to the higher spiritual life of the illuminative stage is often called today a second conversion. Similarly, entrance to the unitive way from the illuminative way is necessarily through an even deeper dark night, the dark night of the spirit. This deeper and passive purgation was seen in the experience of the apostles in the ascension of Jesus, and is recognized today in what is called a third conversion. This deeper purification in the apostles greatly strengthened them, and prepared them for the total personal commitment to the apostolate to which they were sent by Christ.

After reading of the prayers and blessings conferred upon the soul in the higher mansions of St. Teresa, it might be difficult to understand how such a soul would have any need of further purgations. We might similarly be puzzled with the behavior even of the apostles after the resurrection but before Pentecost: how could they still be afraid; why did they still need "power from on high" (Lk 24:49)? Yet the apostles were not perfected even after Christ came to them in His glorified body; still they hid behind locked doors (Jn 20:26, 19).

Fr. Garrigou-Lagrange discusses this topic in a section entitled "The Defects of the Advanced", which enables us to understand the real need for purification even among people of deep mystical experience.[21] Defects remain in persons in the illuminative way, and these defects must be rooted out: God calls us to the perfection of holiness. As the summit of our destiny becomes clearer, so also does the need and the value of the cross which we are commanded to carry daily.

All of us on the path have some sense of God's holiness, and we know of a purgatory to cleanse us before our final entrance into the glorious presence of the Almighty. The clearer our sense of the glory of that encounter, and of the absolute holiness required of us, then the fuller and more profound becomes our sense of unworthiness, and our genuine need of purgatory. Yet purgation need not wait until after death, when it can only cleanse. All purgation that is achieved in this life still leaves time and opportunity for our merit, through acts of charity in Christian living. This last major purgation on earth, offered to us in the dark night of the spirit, has then much in common with the cross, and with purgatory. It is preparation for the presence of God, and it enables in us the holiness and the life of charity which are God's intentions for us.

These purgations of the dark night, which Teresa describes in her sixth mansions, are then both necessary and valuable. They are necessary because of the defects which still remain in the soul at this stage; they are valuable because they enable a charitable life worthy of a Christian. These two benefits of course are not independent: it is precisely those defects in the soul which inhibit or obstruct a true life of charity, directing our concerns selfishly instead of in love. As the soul realizes more and more its own need for correction and cleansing, it grows in appreciation of the Surgeon's precise spiritual scalpel; it begins to embrace lovingly the hard cross sent to it in love.

What are some of these lingering imperfections? Fr. Garrigou-Lagrange, summarizing St. John of the Cross, writes of voluntary distractions in prayer, dullness, useless dissipation, excessive and unenlightened sympathy for specific persons leading to a lack of proper concern for others, excessive attachment to certain spiritual blessings, arrogance and condescension toward other persons. "Thereby, though unaware of it, these advanced souls are puffed up with spiritual pride and presumption and thus deviate from the simplicity, humility, and purity required for close union with God."[22] There remains a deeply rooted self-love which detracts from the relationship which God requires, and which only God can clearly see and remove. These defects He effectively deals with in the passive purgations of the dark night of the spirit. In the suffering He permits, the soul is freed from the attachments and selfish loves which were pulling it down. Under His hand, the soul sees in complete clarity the truth of itself in the light of Almighty God.

It must be stressed that these defects remain prior to the

final purgation even in a truly zealous soul, even in one earnestly striving for the fullness of life with God. Deadly self-love is always maneuvering for benefit and gain, always willing to use religion and sacrifice for its own advancement. This deep wound and disorder in the soul is contrary to the life which the soul at this stage consciously desires. These imperfections render it unable to enter the self-giving divine love of the Trinity. This remaining and deadly mercenary bent in its love is mostly invisible to the soul at this stage, but it becomes visible as it is purged in the fires of divine purgation. Thus the cross becomes the deepest blessing, the most precious gift. It is the cleansing sword of our true Friend, the One willing to hurt for a moment, that He might rejoice with us forever. Thus we begin to know the depths of His love for us, that He does not stop until His work is completed. He does not stop loving us, but brings us into union with Him in the Holy Trinity, which is the deepest desire of our hearts.

The Prayer of Transforming Union:
St. Teresa's Seventh Mansions

Father Garrigou-Lagrange entitles this last stage of prayer "prelude of the union of heaven".[23] This is the summit of prayer attainable on earth, the final stage of the perfect who have advanced through the unitive stage of the spiritual life. In this stage of prayer the soul experiences a profound knowledge of the Trinity, although not to the perfection still anticipated in the beatific vision of God yet to come after death. The soul remains in the order of faith and not vision, but at the clearest and simplest and sweetest supreme pinnacle of faith. St. Teresa describes the seventh mansions as the innermost interior of the soul where God dwells. Arriving there after the trials and purgations of the dark night of the spirit, the soul finds God within itself, as Father, Son, and Holy Spirit. Here spiritual communion is most complete: "The soul sees in the Blessed Trinity an eminent exemplar of Eucharistic Communion, and of the closest union of the soul with its Creator and Father, according to the words of Jesus: 'That they may be one as We also are one.'"[24] This correspondence of Eucharistic Communion with the prayer union of the perfect with God will be discussed further in the chapter on the Mass. The most holy liturgy of the Mass is exactly ordered to our perfection in holiness and charity, being as it is one with the perfect sacrifice of the love of Christ.

The soul so intimately one with Christ will share His peace and joy, yet may also share in His sorrows. As Christ was "sorrowful unto death", so may a soul share in His suffering for the salvation of the world. This intimate union is paralleled in our human experience in the sacrament of marriage, and is called by Teresa the spiritual marriage with the Spouse of our souls. Here the Lord joins the soul to Himself, and enables sweet and most intimate communication. St. Teresa writes, "Here all three Persons communicate themselves to [the soul], speak to it, and explain those words of the Lord in the Gospel: that He and the Father and the Holy Spirit will come to dwell with the soul that loves Him and keeps His commandments."[25]

Teresa lists and discusses several effects in the soul in this stage of prayer, the first being a forgetfulness of self. All the attention of the person is concerned for the honor of God. Teresa writes that the soul would gladly lay down its life and die for even one degree of increase for the glory and honor of God. The second effect is the desire in the soul for suffering, in union with the suffering Christ. This desire was also in previous mansions, but now it is more peaceful than before, accompanied with a stronger desire for the complete will of God. To suffer or not to suffer is no longer so important as the simple fulfillment of the will of God. Any persecution is met with great interior joy, and with only love for the persecutors. There is no fear of death, nor desire for spiritual consolations or delights. The presence of the Lord is sufficient, giving great detachment from anything else except God, and the salvation of souls for God's sake. Teresa writes that when such a soul becomes distracted, the Lord awakens it with great gentleness, and with tender love.[26]

Conclusion to the Chapter

The ordinary path to holiness is a path of devotion through prayer. We can consider the journey in three major stages of the spiritual life, and we can consider it as seven interior mansions within the soul. In the one image and in the other we see characteristic marks of living and praying: we see that our *life*, in the fullest sense of the word, is a developing relationship with God and a journey toward Him. We cannot describe our life without describing our prayer, nor can we describe our prayer without describing our manner of living. Our personal expression of life is characterized in our interior prayer as well as in our exterior "prayer", which is our manner of living. Our prayer, and our way of living, are two expressions of one relationship with God.

God enables us to grow toward Him in stages. How can we cooperate with this truth? We cannot instantly become a saint, any more than a child can instantly become a mature adult. But a child can cooperate with his wiser elders and parents, and respond to the genuine love in his home. So too can we see and respond to the authentic love in the Church of Christ. We can receive it and grow in it, into adolescence and on into our own spiritual adulthood.

Prayer that is Effective

Every Christian is edified in praying the prayer taught us by Christ Himself. This prayer has been called the "most perfect of prayers" by St. Thomas Aquinas, quoted in the *Catechism of the Catholic Church*.[27] Acknowledging the recognition of Tertullian, the Church affirms that this prayer "is truly the summary of the whole gospel."[28] The *Catechism* has much to say[29] in its final Part Four concerning this remarkable prayer, much that is beautiful and enlightening to us. For the purposes of this book, however, it is helpful to observe how the prayer might align with the three spiritual stages. Observing this, we learn something of God's supernatural work in us as we persevere in prayer through our growth and discipleship. The relationship of the Our Father to the stages of prayer is suggested in Table 3 below.

Table 3	
Stages of Prayer	**The Our Father**
The Unitive Stage, the perfect. (St. Teresa's 6th and 7th mansions.)	Our Father, who art in heaven, hallowed be Thy name. Thy kingdom come,
The Illuminative Stage, the proficient. (St. Teresa's 4th and 5th mansions.)	Thy will be done on earth as it is in heaven. Give us this day our daily bread
The Purgative Stage, the beginner. (St. Teresa's 1st, 2nd and 3rd mansions.)	and forgive us our trespasses as we forgive those who trespass against us. Lead us not into temptation but deliver us from evil. Amen.

As we pray, especially in the beginning stage, our prayer concerns more exterior matters than deeply interior ones. We are indeed unable to see into the interior of our own soul; it is dark and hidden to us. Our conscious concerns are more outward and exterior, having to do initially with our physical needs, and most importantly with our struggle with obvious sins and our need for forgiveness and grace. We see in the Our Father that this area of concern is the last of the petitions of the prayer.

A person having entered the illuminative stage has begun a new relationship with the Lord, and has begun to deal with more interior matters within himself. His concern with material and earthly matters is greatly simplified. His struggle with sin is now more with venial and hidden sins, and with the human imperfections which hinder his imitation of Christ. He has begun to imitate the virtues he treasures. His great concern is for fidelity within his own heart. We see in the Our Father that this is the matter of the second group of petitions.

One who has entered the unitive stage is in most intimate heart-relationship with Christ. With simple confidence he knows filial relationship with his Father. A life of sacrificial worship, of loving self-donation, is his fervent desire. His struggle against sin is within the most interior places of his being, with human imperfections that only further his own humility and magnify the glory of the Lord. In Christ he wages war against the evil one, and knows the certainty of that one's defeat. This Christian calls out to "our Father" in the complete assurance of a son or daughter; with single-hearted intention he prays for the coming of His kingdom. We observe that this petition is the very first group in the prayer taught by Jesus.

What is the meaning of this sequence of petitions, exactly reversed from what we might expect? If we were to make up a prayer, we might begin with the exterior matters of need, and seek to "work our way in," so to speak. We might omit altogether the more interior matters and concerns within the soul, being in fact obscured and hidden from us. Yet Christ has left a prayer for us, left to model and form all our prayers, which is ordered "from the inside out." In the Our Father, Jesus enables us to put into words all the needs of our interior life, even to the most interior and hidden mysteries of our relationship to God in Him. In Christ we can truly call God "Father"! Long before we can deeply understand this, we can verbalize it. Long before it is the central identifying mark of our being, we pray it. In the Our Father, we pray our way into the mysteries of life in Christ, from *within*. The wonderful sequence of petitions of this prayer, and their relationship to the *Interior Castle* of St. Teresa, is the subject of the next chapter.

Notes

[1]   Jordan Aumann, *Spiritual Theology* (Allen, TX: Christian Classics, 1980), 316.

[2]   Aumann, 320 ff.

[3]   I first was introduced to this method by Fr. William J. Mountain, S.J. in a series of retreats he led in the 1970's.

[4]   An excellent little book on this subject is *Lectio Divina: An Ancient Prayer That Is Ever New* by Mario Masini, trans. Edmund C. Lane, S.S.P. (New York: ST PAULS/ Alba House, 1998).

[5]   St. Teresa of Avila, *Interior Castle*, 1:1 [St. Teresa of Avila, *The Collected Works of St. Teresa of Avila*, trans. Kieran Kavanaugh O.C.D. and Otilio Rodriguez, O.C.D. (Washington, DC: ICS Publications, 1980), 283].

[6]   *Interior Castle*, 286.

[7]   Ibid., 316.

[8]   Garrigou-Lagrange, *Three Ages*, vol. 2, p. 41.

[9]   *The Dark Night*, Book I, chapter 9 [St. John of the Cross, *The Collected Works of St. John of the Cross*, trans. Kieran Kavanaugh O.C.D. and Otilio Rodriguez, O.C.D. (Washington, DC: ICS Publications, 1973), 313-16].

[10]   Garrigou-Lagrange, *Three Ages,* vol. 2, p. 51.

[11]   St. Teresa of Avila, *Interior Castle*, 332.

[12]   Ibid., 336.

[13]   Ibid., 338.

[14]   Ibid., 339.

[15] Ibid., 347.
[16] Ibid., 353.
[17] Ibid., 355.
[18] Ibid., 359.
[19] Ibid., 362.
[20] Ibid., 366.
[21] Garrigou-Lagrange, *Three Ages*, vol. 2, p. 358.
[22] Ibid.
[23] Garrigou-Lagrange, *Three Ages*, vol. 2, p. 527.
[24] Ibid., p. 529.
[25] St. Teresa, *Interior Castle*, 430; cf. Jn 14:23.
[26] Ibid., 440.
[27] *Catechism of the Catholic Church*, 2763.
[28] Ibid., 2761.
[29] Ibid., 2761-2865.

CHAPTER FIVE

THE OUR FATHER, AND THE INTERIOR CASTLE OF ST. TERESA

The Seven Petitions of the Our Father

The seven petitions of the Our Father are related in a surprising but beautiful way to the interior journey of the soul as seen by St. Teresa of Jesus (of Avila). There is a special appropriateness of each of the seven petitions of the Our Father to its corresponding dwelling within the soul: the seven petitions to the seven interior mansions. Through this correspondence, we come to understand more deeply the completeness and perfection of the divine prayer, and we come to appreciate more fully the supernatural insights granted St. Teresa. This is of great benefit, if then we come to pray and to live more worthy and faithful Christian lives.

The Our Father is a prayer of infinite worth and scope. In this chapter, an aspect of the prayer that is stressed is that it is a priestly prayer, a prayer of intercession for the whole Church. It is an expression of the priesthood of Christ, prayed for all for whom He came and died. In commending this prayer to us, He commanded us into His priesthood and His kenosis. In the se-

131

quence of the petitions of the prayer, we gain insight into His divine perspective as eternal high priest — indeed, we enter into His perspective.

This prayer is directly relevant, as well, to our personal vocation: to the journey of the soul to holiness. This aspect of the prayer is stressed as well in this chapter: this is the prayer of our journey. These two aspects of the prayer are linked: our personal vocation to holiness is linked essentially to our share in the priesthood of Christ. These two are inseparable. That is, our journey to holiness is a journey into divine charity, holy love. Holy love finds its fullness in self-gift, the emblem of which is the cross of our Lord.

Introduction

> Our Father who art in heaven,
> Hallowed be Thy name.
> Thy kingdom come.
> Thy will be done,
> On earth as it is in heaven.
> Give us this day our daily bread;
> And forgive us our trespasses,
> As we forgive those who trespass against us.
> And lead us not into temptation,
> But deliver us from evil.

The Our Father is much more than a prayer; it is more than a model prayer and more even than *the* model prayer. The Our Father is the very essence of prayer, including within itself all prayer and omitting nothing that is prayer. All prayer that is true prayer is a participation in this prayer. All true prayer is a sharing in this, the full and essential prayer.

The Our Father can be called the perfect prayer. Its perfection comes from the perfection of its historical source, Jesus Christ: we can be sure that His prayer is perfect. When we pray this prayer, we not only imitate Him, but we enter into communion with Him. Our Lord did not say for us to pray "your Father," but "our Father." That is, we pray this prayer not only in obedience to Christ the Son of God, which is reason enough, but with Him in His sacred humanity. In this prayer we are invited to a participation in His prayer, and so in His priesthood, interceding with Him for ourselves and for all the Church. In union with the Church and in Him we pray to our Father.

The power of this prayer comes from its source within us as we pray. Within us, the Holy Trinity dwells. Within us, the Son is speaking His eternal prayer of communion, "Father!" The prayer itself calls us to this source, the interior communion of the Trinity.

At first glance a great tension appears between "Our Father," which evokes a profound nearness, and "who art in heaven," which points far beyond us. This tension between most near and most distant, between immediate and completely other, is resolved only in the great mystery of the dignity of the human person: we are created beings, created out of nothing, yet created in the image of God!

The source of this prayer, as we pray it, is not merely our lips or mind or memory, but the Word Himself, professing. It is His word, His prayer given to become our confession with Him. The *Catechism of the Catholic Church* (CCC) assures us, "When we pray to the Father, we are in communion with Him and with His Son, Jesus Christ" (CCC, 2781). Christ prays this prayer within us, and we with Him, in the most interior center of our souls. The *Catechism* quotes St. Peter Chrysologus, "When would a mortal dare call God 'Father,' if man's innermost being were not animated by power from on high?" (CCC, 2777).

Our communion with the Son enables our sonship: we have a participation in the filial relationship of Christ to His Father. It is because and only because by grace we are in Him, that we can say with Him "our Father." Again, the *Catechism* explains this: "…the Spirit of the Son grants a participation in that very relationship to us who believe that Jesus is the Christ and that we are born of God" (CCC, 2780).

He, in the Blessed Trinity, indwells us and prays in unceasing intercession for us the Church. We read in Scripture, "Jesus' priesthood is permanent because He remains forever. Thus He is able for all time to bring complete salvation to those who approach God through Him, since He is always alive to intercede for them" (Heb 7:24-25). Because the source of this prayer is Christ, we can see the correspondence of this prayer with the essential expression of the priesthood of Christ: His kenosis in love, His passion. Because the source of this prayer is Christ most interior within our souls, we can see the correspondence of this prayer with the needs, the journey, the history, the formation, the transformation of the soul. We may see this latter correspondence perhaps most easily through the seven mansions, the transformation-journey of the soul described by St. Teresa of Avila in *The Interior Castle.*

When we pray this prayer, then, we give echo to His petition on our behalf for our sanctification; and we join with Him in His loving praise of His eternal Father, now by grace our Father also. Our Christ, His Son, prays this prayer now, within us, in the innermost interior of the human soul. He chooses to remain there, indwelling a created spirit made in His image: three divine Persons in eternal communion, in divine loving relationship, within the human soul. There in us is this prayer forever offered to the Father; in our confession with Him we enter His priestly love-communion.

The Prayer

The preeminent place of the Lord's Prayer in our life of prayer is taught by the Church. Following Tertullian, she proclaims that it is "truly the summit of the whole Gospel" (CCC, 2761). The beautiful exposition of the prayer given in the *Catechism* will not be repeated here, but anyone could benefit greatly by meditation and reflection on that presentation. In this chapter we will develop the mystery of the *sequence* of petitions given in this prayer, and relate this sequence to the "Interior Castle" seen by St. Teresa.

St. Thomas saw the importance of the sequence of petitions:

> The Lord's Prayer is the most perfect of prayers.... In it we ask, not only for all the things we can rightly desire, but also in the sequence that they should be desired. This prayer not only teaches us to ask for things, but also in what order we should desire them.[1]   (CCC, 2763)

In the sequence of petitions in the Our Father we find the mystery of the Absolute speaking from within His fallen creation. In the Our Father, we see the divine movement *from* the center and ground of our being in His Being, *out to* the distant fringes of our estrangement from Him. It is like the net thrown into the sea: beginning in His mouth and near His heart, He casts to the outermost reaches of our need, and then gathers them back to Himself. The net begins with the closest, and proceeds to the most separated, and gathers again. It is also like the radiation of light from within the supernatural crystal of the soul: beginning at its source in the innermost center of the

Castle (as Teresa saw the soul), the light radiates out, through the interior dwelling places, until all is illuminated.

The divine character of the Our Father is demonstrated in this sequence! A prayer of human origin would probably not proceed in this way, but rather, in all likelihood, in the opposite sequence. We would probably begin our prayer with our struggle against evil, and with temptation, praying for His strength. We would place our needs before Him, only gradually hoping for our hope against all hope, that we might be with Him and in Him and for Him with all our lives. We would begin with "Lord, deliver us from evil!," and develop our way in prayer to eventually cry out at the end that God might be "our Father" also. The prayer taught us by Jesus does not proceed in this way.

In the prayer given us by Jesus, we begin with the end. We begin our prayer with the declaration "Our Father," an assertion so awesome that we continue to pray only by supernatural grace itself, unless we are so deaf to our own words that we recite as in a stupor. We begin with this word of divine relationship and communion — our end and God's intention — and from there proceed outwardly, so to speak, outwardly through the path that we must travel if we are to reach that end, until we come to the end of the prayer and the beginning of our journey: "deliver us from evil."

From the human perspective our salvation begins after Baptism with our struggle against evil. After He was baptized Jesus was led by the Spirit into the wilderness to be tempted by the Devil. In the traditional Catholic spiritual understanding of the journey of the soul, from beginner in the purgative stage to proficient in the illuminative stage to the perfect in the unitive stage,[2] we begin with a struggle against sin, even mortal sin. In this traditional view if we advance in the Christian life it is toward our final end in Christ, communion and divine fellowship in Him, perfection in charity which is divine life. It is in this end that the profession "Our Father" is consummated, made fully meaningful, and finally understood.

What, then, does this divinely given sequence mean for us? What does it tell us? Why has our Lord told us, "Pray then like this"? Since this prayer has its source in divine mystery itself, in the mission of the Son and in His priestly offering to the Father, this mystery will not be exhausted here! The mystery of the sequence is, I believe, at least this: it is an invitation into the mission of the Son; it is a participation in His journey from the Father, into separation and death, so to speak, and back again.

The Interior Castle:
The Seven Petitions and the Seven Mansions

This journey is more clearly seen, perhaps, through the vision of the soul given to St. Teresa, the Interior Castle.[3] In the seven mansions Teresa saw seven dwellings of the soul, within the soul, in the journey of the soul toward its end the Holy Trinity. While cautioning against a simplistic reading or thoughts of a linear progression — as though step 1 leads next to step 2, and so on — Teresa insisted that "You mustn't think of these dwelling places in such a way that each one would follow in file after the other; but turn your eyes toward the center, which is the room or royal chamber where the King stays...."[4] Rather, surrounding the center are many rooms above, below, to the right and to the left, so to speak. Yet by seven concentric layers of rooms, as a sphere divided into seven concentric layers of shells, Teresa's insight into the soul may be pictured. Hence the "first mansions" are all those rooms most distant from the center and from the King who dwells in that center. Those first rooms share certain common temptations and certain graces, certain prayers and certain dangers, which Teresa describes. The next "layer" of rooms, so to speak, the "second mansions" also share certain common features which she describes, and so on. Thus she continues describing the soul, and increasingly the prayer of the soul, as the soul journeys toward the innermost (seventh) mansions where God dwells.

The mansions are here described in the order they are encountered by the soul, as the soul journeys toward God. To align the petitions of the prayer with the journey of the soul, the seven petitions are discussed in reverse order.

The 1st Mansions — "But deliver us from evil"

Souls in the first mansions of its journey are in special and grave danger, having just escaped from the clutches of the evil one. Teresa writes,

> since in the first rooms souls are still absorbed in the world and engulfed in their pleasures and vanities, with their honors and pretenses, their vassals (which are these senses and faculties) don't have the strength God gave human nature in the beginning. And these souls are easily conquered, even though they may go about with desires not to offend God and though they do perform good works. Those who see themselves in this state must approach His majesty as often as possible. They must take His Blessed Mother and His saints as intercessors so that these intercessors may fight for them, for the soul's vassals have little strength to defend themselves.[5]

The last petition of the Our Father is uniquely needed in these dwellings, then, since the soul is especially vulnerable and weak. Teresa stresses the need to grow in self-knowledge, of the horror and ugliness of all sin, and to grow also in the realization of the sublime beauty of the soul. These needs are addressed in the full prayer of the Our Father, yet in the last petition of the prayer is the unique and urgent need of the soul: deliver us! The whole Church, then, in praying this prayer, asks not only for their own needs for deliverance, which may be more or less urgent, but also joins in the saving priesthood of Christ in petitioning for the "very least" of His brethren. In this communion of priests, we live our vocation and pray "*our* Father."

The 2nd Mansions —
"And lead us not into temptation"

These are souls who have grown somewhat in sensitivity to spiritual matters, and who are now somewhat more receptive to the graces and prompting of God. They are those "who have understood how important it is not to stay in the first dwelling places. But they still don't have the determination to remain in this second stage without turning back, for they don't avoid the occasion of sin. This failure to avoid these occasions is quite dangerous."[6]

This is a time when "perseverance is most necessary," Teresa writes. "The attacks made by devils in a thousand ways afflict the soul more in these rooms than in the previous ones." The devils "bring to mind the esteem one has in the world, one's friends and relatives, one's health (when there's thought of penitential practices, for the soul that enters this dwelling place always begins wanting to practice some penance) and a thousand other obstacles."[7]

Souls in these second mansions are in grave danger in the near occasions of sin, and so have special and urgent need for protection against the subtleties of temptation. Teresa writes, "Ah, my Lord! Your help is necessary here; without it one can do nothing. In Your mercy do not consent to allow this soul to suffer deception and give up what was begun."[8] Hence we see the special need, for souls in these rooms, to petition for deliverance from temptation! The whole Church prays this, however: "lead *us* not into temptation." In priestly intercession for others, and in special priestly intercession for those most in need, the whole Church with one voice offers this petition to our Lord. None would be presumptuous enough to think he is in no danger in temptation! All pray this in sincerity of heart! Yet in priestly intercession all join in support of all, as we pray "our Father."

The 3rd Mansions — "And forgive us our trespasses, as we forgive those who have trespassed against us"

Souls who have entered the third dwellings in the interior journey have made great progress. They are very sensitive to the offenses against God that sin inflicts. They are keen to the ugliness of even venial sins, and seek ascetical practices and works of worship of God. Their prayer, while still ascetical and not mystical, is simpler and more frequent. Teresa writes,

> They long not to offend His Majesty, even guarding themselves against venial sins; they are fond of doing penance and setting aside periods of recollection; they spend their time well, practicing works of charity toward their neighbors; and are very balanced in their use of speech and dress and in the governing of their households — those who have them.[9]

Teresa warns, however, against dangers of this dwelling which come from a lack of right humility. The practice of virtue may lead to an excess of self-confidence. When dryness in prayer or other trials come, such persons may become very troubled. "When humility is present, this stage is a most excellent one. If humility is lacking, we will remain here all our life — and with a thousand afflictions and miseries."[10] She counsels,

> Let us look at our own faults and leave aside those of others, for it is very characteristic of persons with such well-ordered lives to be shocked by everything. Perhaps we could truly learn from the one who shocks us what is most important even though we may surpass him in external composure and our way of dealing with others.[11]

This third petition of the Our Father, which links a plea for mercy with the need for justice, links also the special need for souls in these mansions for generous forgiveness of others, and humble admission of personal fault. Teresa points out the critical need in these mansions to "look at our own faults" and "leave aside those of others," hence "forgive us, as we have forgiven." Here again, it is not that this petition of the Our Father is only for some and not for all of the Church! We all have need to pray this petition: it is truth. Even those not having urgent or immediate personal need of this plea, however, if there could be any, have need by virtue of communion to pray it for the whole Church. Because He is our Father, we must pray for the whole Church, having been gathered ourselves into the priesthood and the cross of Christ.

The 4th Mansions — "Give us this day our daily bread"

The fourth mansions in the journey of the soul mark a radical and essential change. In the fourth mansions, the soul advances beyond ascetical prayer — attainable through ordinary grace — and enters mystical prayer through genuinely supernatural experience. God grants a work in the soul beyond those consolations sometimes given in ascetical prayer: He grants what Teresa calls spiritual delight.[12] The effect of this supernatural work of delight is to "expand the heart," enabling the love which is our vocation. Yet Teresa must say,

> One strong warning I give to whoever finds himself in this state is that he guard very carefully against placing himself in the occasion of offending God. In this prayer the soul is not yet grown but is like a suckling child. If it turns away from its mother's breasts, what can be expected for it but death? I am very afraid that this will happen to anyone to whom God has granted this favor and who withdraws from prayer — unless he does so for a particularly special reason — or if he doesn't return quickly to prayer he will go from bad to worse. I know there is a great deal to fear in this matter.[13]

The need Teresa writes for those in these mansions, the need for "its mother's breasts" to grow and become strengthened in its new relationship with His Majesty, is reflected in the fourth petition of the Our Father for "our daily bread." The soul in these mansions is in urgent need of spiritual sustenance. While this petition of the prayer can rightly be applied to our material needs in this life, it carries the deeper petition for that heavenly bread which is the Eucharist. The soul in these mansions needs the food of eternal life! It has just been awakened in him, so to speak, in the experiences of infused contemplation. He has come into a second conversion; he has awakened to the presence of the Lord in a most real, personal, and authentic way. But he is now in unique danger, which Teresa alerts us to. This soul must become nourished at the breast of his mother. Mother Church must provide that nourishment, as she does, in her most precious meal. Our bread includes material needs, and material food, but most importantly our bread is that of the spirit: all that is for the Church is for us, and most urgently for those at the threshold of the mystical life. In this petition the whole Church sends up her epiclesis ("invocation," the intercessory prayer asking the Father to send the Holy Spirit), awaiting the response of the Spirit. We live our priesthood uniquely in this petition, interceding for all and especially for those most in need, for the bread to feed us.

The 5th Mansions — "Thy will be done, on earth as it is in heaven"

The relationship to God of the soul in this dwelling is the relationship of union, specifically with God's will. Teresa calls the prayer of these mansions the prayer of union. In speaking of the deep spiritual delights of this union, Teresa writes, "One cannot arrive at the delightful union if the union coming from being resigned to God's will is not very certain. Oh, how desirable is this union with God's will! Happy the soul that has reached it."[14]

Teresa writes that there is no great difficulty in discerning the will of God! His will is simple: our perfection in charity, "love of His Majesty and love of our neighbor."[15] Our love for

God, Teresa writes, is less certain to ourselves than our love for neighbor: love for neighbor is demonstrable. "We cannot know whether or not we love God, although there are strong indications for recognizing that we do love Him; but we can know whether we love our neighbor. And be certain that the more advanced you see you are in love for your neighbor the more advanced you will be in the love of God"[16]

In the perfection of love we fully live within His will. As Teresa describes it we move toward, in this fifth dwelling place, the perfecting of covenantal love in marriage. In this fifth dwelling is the "meeting," the "joining of hands" with the divine Spouse.[17] It is reserved to the sixth dwelling to make firm the betrothal with our Spouse, and to the seventh, the spiritual marriage itself.

The fifth petition is meaningful to all in His Church, from the youngest novice to the most advanced elder. Yet to those in the fifth mansions, this petition is newly and urgently meaningful. The personal will of the souls in these mansions is newly one, in mystical prayer, with the will of God. His will is now known in a most personal and intimate way, although even now not completely, because the journey is not even now complete. But the soul embraces in a way it has never before known, the holy will of God. The will of God has become the will of the soul, and the soul most generously proclaims "thy will be done!"

Teresa describes this profound union with His will:

> It sees within itself a desire to praise the Lord; it would want to dissolve and die a thousand deaths for Him. It soon begins to experience a desire to suffer great trials without its being able to do otherwise. There are the strongest desires for penance, for solitude, and that all might know God; and great pain comes to it when it sees that He is offended.[18]

In this deep union with God the soul in these mansions prays "thy will be done."

The 6th Mansions — "Thy kingdom come"

This dwelling, as Teresa describes it, is an experience of profound suffering and of joy in Christ, to whom the soul becomes betrothed. After elaborating on both of these favors, the suffering and the joy, she writes "Our Lord grants these favors to the soul because, as to one to whom He is truly betrothed, one who is already determined to do His will in everything, He desires to give it some knowledge of how to do His will and of His grandeurs."[19] Through both the suffering and the flights of spiritual ecstasy, with imaginative visions, the soul becomes almost completely detached from any love for this world. This detachment comes through joy: "The joy makes a person so forgetful of self and of all things that he doesn't advert to, nor can he speak of anything other than the praises of God which proceed from his joy."[20] The detachment comes also through the suffering: "The soul is left with greater contempt for the world than before because it sees that nothing in the world was any help to it in that torment, and it is much more detached from creatures because it now sees that only the Creator can console and satisfy it."[21]

The soul in these sixth mansions prays in a uniquely meaningful way, then, "Thy kingdom come." The whole Church prays this petition in the midst of the Our Father, and calls upon Him to send and establish His reign. Yet the souls in the sixth mansions, having endured and grown in loving intimacy and obedience, pray this petition in a simplicity which calls us to remember the fiat of Mary: "Be it done unto me according to your word." These souls are betrothed to the Lord! They are given to Him through the sufferings and the ecstasies of kenosis: a self-donation that is a participation in the passion of Christ. We all pray this prayer, and all of this prayer; we pray for ourselves, and we pray for the whole Church. With Christ, we become priests and shepherds, gathering His people into His kingdom.

The 7th Mansions — "Our Father who art in heaven, hallowed be Thy name"

> When our Lord is pleased to have pity on this soul that He has already taken spiritually as His Spouse because of what it suffers and has suffered through its desires, He brings it, before the spiritual marriage is consummated, into His dwelling place which is this seventh mansion. For just as in heaven so in the soul His Majesty must have a room where He dwells alone. Let us call it another heaven.[22]

In this dwelling, the soul is brought into spiritual marriage with the Lord, sharing, in a special personal sense, in His holy name. Here Teresa describes the supreme intimacy of the soul with the Beloved, this side of the Beatific Vision. In this dwelling,

> the Most Blessed Trinity, through an intellectual vision, is revealed to it through a certain representation of the truth. Here all three Persons communicate themselves to it, speak to it, and explain those words of the Lord in the Gospel: that He and the Father and the Holy Spirit will come to dwell with the soul that loves Him and keeps His commandments.[23]

In this dwelling the presence of the Trinity within the soul is revealed and assured, and our Baptism "in the name of the Father, and of the Son, and of the Holy Spirit" is perfected. Here the holy name is hallowed in the interior worship and love of the soul, now wed with her Spouse. The holy name is hallowed here in a most human and personal way, and in a most complete way. Here the prayer of the soul is most fully united with the love-communion of Father and Son, in the Spirit. All souls can and should pray this prayer and this petition of the prayer, "asking the Father that His name be made holy" (CCC, 2807). The soul brought by His grace to this dwelling is enabled to pray this petition with Him, *in His name*, in a union so close that Teresa describes it as sacramental and covenantal: that is, in the bond of marriage. Yet the whole Church, praying through grace and in faith "beyond ourselves" so to speak, pray toward this union in the holiness of His name.

How can we ever, as we pray, move beyond the sublime meanings contained in these opening words of the prayer? How can we continue to speak, having confessed with the Son this divine communion? St. Teresa wondered this perhaps in the year 1566, writing in *The Way of Perfection* these beautiful opening words,[24]

This favor would not be so great, Lord, if it came at the end of the prayer. But at the beginning, You fill our hands and give a reward so large that it would easily fill the intellect and thus occupy the will in such a way one would be unable to speak a word. Oh daughters! how readily should perfect contemplation come at this point![25]

Conclusion to the Chapter

There is of necessity great mystery in the sequence of petitions of the Our Father, because of its divine origin. Yet we can see somewhat into the mystery through the writings of St. Teresa, Doctor of the Church. Her understanding of the journey of the soul, from its first responses to the Gospel to its ultimate loving union with Christ in spiritual marriage, gives us a framework in which to reconsider this traditional prayer. With a correspondence that is difficult to deny, we come to see in a fresh way the divine wisdom that it holds.

The Our Father is a prayer that we can pray only in Christ and with Him, because it is His priestly prayer of intercession and ingathering for all His people. His prayer begins in Himself, in His love-communion with the Father, yet we are under obedience to offer His words with Him. His words, active and living with the Spirit, begin with our end in Him, "Our Father who art in heaven!" The prayer ends in what is for fallen humanity the beginning of our journey, "deliver us from evil." Our prayer *with* Him is our *participation with Him* as priest and shepherd, building His Church.

In the prayer Our Father, we reach toward the blessed communion of love in the Holy Trinity. We pray with the Son who most intimately shares that life; we confess with Him and mysteriously share His fellowship: "our Father." In that confession, gathered into His priestly intercession, in union with the whole Church, we recite the perfect petitions of the perfect prayer.

Our vocation requires a journey, for we are not where we are called to be. We are on a path, traveled by St. Teresa and well described by her *Interior Castle*. To the extent that we reach toward the beatitude of our end, we reach not for ourselves alone but in priestly intercession with Christ for all. This is indeed the perfect prayer, the whole Gospel summed. With Him in prayer we strengthen ourselves and one another, calling down graces for our journey as Church into His perfect communion. Each recitation of the Our Father carries us through the journey, from end to beginning. Each time we pray "in this way" we enter the movement of the Spirit sent out from communion in the Trinity, so to speak to the very least of His brethren. The Our Father recounts the mission of Christ and calls us into it. The Our Father forms us into His Body, His apostolate, His cross, His life.

The *Catechism* directs us to the *end* of our journey, a journey so well described by St. Teresa. The *Catechism* paragraph closes with a prayer that expresses much that was attempted in this chapter.

> The ultimate end of the whole divine economy is the entry of God's creatures into the perfect unity of the Blessed Trinity. But even now we are called to be a dwelling for the Most Holy Trinity: "If a man loves me," says the Lord, "he will keep my word, and my Father will love him, and we will come to him, and make our home with him" (Jn 14:23):
>
> O my God, Trinity whom I adore, help me forget myself entirely so to establish myself in you, unmovable and peaceful as if my soul were already in eternity. May nothing be able to trouble my peace or make me leave you, O my unchanging God, but may each minute bring me more deeply into your mystery! Grant my soul peace. Make it your heaven, your beloved dwelling and the place of your rest. May I never abandon you there, but may I be there, whole and entire, completely vigilant in my faith, entirely adoring, and wholly given over to your creative action. (Prayer of Blessed Elizabeth of the Trinity)
>
> (CCC, 260)

Notes

1 St. Thomas Aquinas, *Summa*, II-II, 83, 9.

2 For example, cf. Reginald Garrigou-Lagrange, O.P., *The Three Ages of the Interior Life*, (Rockford, IL: Tan Books, 1989).

3 All references to *Interior Castle* or *The Way of Perfection* are from *The Collected Works of St. Teresa of Avila*, tr. K. Kavanaugh, O.C.D., and O. Rodriguez, O.C.D. (Washington DC: Institute of Carmelite Studies, 1980), vol. II.

4 *Interior Castle*, I:2, 8.

5 Ibid., I:2, 12.

6 Ibid., II:1, 2.

7 Ibid., II:1, 3.

8 Ibid., II:1, 6.

9 Ibid., III:1, 5.

10 Ibid., III:2, 9.

11 Ibid., III:2, 13.

12 Ibid., IV:1, 4.

13 Ibid., IV:3, 10.

14 Ibid., V:3, 3.

15 Ibid., V:3, 7.

16 Ibid., V:3, 8.

17 Ibid., V:4, 4.

18 Ibid., V:2, 7.

19 Ibid., VI:10, 8.

20 Ibid., VI:7, 13.

21 Ibid., VI:11, 10.

22 Ibid., VII:1, 3.

23 Ibid., VII:1, 6.

24 In *The Way of Perfection* Teresa explained the petitions of the Our Father in relation to the grades of prayer as she then understood them. In that work she related the petitions in the order they are prayed, to the increasing grades of prayer as they are encountered in the soul. The strange reality that our spiritual end is prayed in the beginning was noted by Teresa, as quoted, but she continued to apply the prayer as she had begun. Eleven years later, in 1577, she had finished *Interior Castle*, and her description of the seven mansions. We can only wonder what she would have written concerning the Our Father, had she continued writing.

25 *The Way of Perfection*, 27:1.

CHAPTER SIX

GROWING IN HOLINESS: THE SACRAMENTS

Catholic Sacramental Life

The Catholic Church and the Orthodox churches are sacramental! In the apostolic church traditions (those traceable back to the apostles of Christ), sacraments hold an intimate and essential place. The sacramentality of the Catholic Church, in particular, is one of her outwardly distinguishing marks amid the many Protestant churches around her. There is something of a range of attitudes about sacraments among churches of the Reformed tradition, but the sacraments are for Catholics the means of our vocation: within the sacramental life of the Church we enter the path and are nurtured along the journey to holiness in Christ. The *Catechism of the Catholic Church* teaches:

> The fruit of sacramental life is both personal and ecclesial. For every one of the faithful on the one hand, this fruit is life for God in Christ Jesus; for the Church, on the other, it is an increase in charity and in her mission of witness.[1]

151

Life, for a Catholic Christian, is Christ. The essential christocentricity of our faith is in no way opposed by our devotion to the sacraments — rather, every one of our sacraments is a unique encounter with Christ. Our Christian life begins when we become *in* Jesus Christ, by the grace of God. This change is first of all a change due to the unmerited grace of God: "For by grace you have been saved through faith, and this is God's gift; it didn't come from you" (Eph 2:8). Secondly, this change is a transformation which begins with a translation: in the sacrament of Baptism, which is the sacrament of faith, we are translated *out of* the old Adam of sin, and *into* the second Adam of grace, the Christ.

It is *in* Christ that we are saved. Our whole Christian vocation is concerned then with remaining in Him, growing into holiness in Him, and living our lives in Him. "*He* is the source of your life *in Christ Jesus*, whom God made our wisdom, our righteousness and sanctification and redemption" (1 Cor 1:30, italics added). When we come to really understand that our calling is to remain and to live *in Him*, then much of the confusion we may have experienced in our earlier days as a Christian disappears.

A different perspective is held by some of our Protestant brothers and sisters, who believe that we are not truly transformed, but rather are covered by Christ and His Blood. That is, some Protestants are taught that we are made acceptable to the Father by this divine covering, but we remain sinful creatures as we were before. They believe that now the Father cannot see our sin and its ugliness because of this covering of Christ. This error arises because of their misunderstandings about justification itself, and original sin. The Catholic Church holds, however, that in fact we are deeply and truly transformed by the grace of God in Baptism. "Therefore, anyone who is in

Christ is a new creation; the old has passed away, behold the new has come!" (2 Cor 5:17).

It is prudent to keep aware of this difference when talking with Protestant friends, or when listening to Protestant teachings, in case this or related errors come to the surface. Of course there is no one Protestant theology: if there were, there would be only one Protestant church. Nor is error limited to our Protestant brothers and sisters! Much error is held as true today even by Catholics, and errors are being passed on because of a lack of clear teaching of the truths handed down to the Church. The resultant confusion is an obstacle to both personal spiritual growth and the unity of God's people. Our Lord wants unity among us; we are called by the Church to do all that we can to encourage real ecumenism. Essential to unity, of course, is faithfulness to the truth.

There are seven sacraments given to the Church. In this chapter, we will consider five of the seven sacraments: those five which are immediately important to most Catholics in their daily journey. We will consider especially the personal relevance of these five in our daily path to holiness and maturity in Christ: Baptism, Confirmation, Eucharist, Penance, and Matrimony. The Sacrament of Holy Orders will be discussed, although not as fully as it deserves, in Chapter 7.[2] The Sacrament of the Anointing of the Sick will be considered in Chapter 8, when we discuss the matter of suffering and dying.[3]

Our sacramental journey as Catholics begins with our entrance into Life, into Christ, through Baptism. We are strengthened for Christian maturity by the Sacrament of Confirmation. We are spiritually fed and nourished throughout the journey in the Sacrament of Holy Eucharist. When we fall, we are forgiven and reestablished in Him through the Sacrament of Reconciliation. Those of us who enter the married state are graced

sacramentally to encounter Christ and His love through the covenantal love of Matrimony. With these five sacraments, we personally embrace our healing and uplifting Lord in five specific,
special ways. In Him we meet our vocation.

Catholic Sacramental Perspective

The Catholic religion is essentially sacramental. This sacramental character is possible, first of all, because of the integrity of our Creator: He made all things consistent with Himself.
Through His integrity, all created reality bears His signature,
and is in some way a sign of Himself.[4] We can hear the Hebrew
recognition of God's word in creation, for example, in the Psalm
passage "The earth, O Lord, is full of Your steadfast love; teach
me Your statutes!" (Ps 119:64). It is simply impossible for the
heavens not to declare God's glory (cf. Ps 19:1). We find ourselves surrounded by such signs of God, which therefore make
all of us accountable to the Truth. We are surrounded by, immersed in, God's self-revelation:

> ...what can be known about God is evident to them,
> since God has revealed it to them. From the creation
> of the world God's invisible attributes — namely, His
> eternal power and divine nature — have been acces-
> sible to human knowledge through created things.
> So they have no excuse....   Rm 1:19-20

All of creation can be considered, if loosely, "sacramental," and signifying in some way the creator God. All realities
are an expression, a "word" of God, which "provides men with
constant evidence of Himself in created realities."[5] In this way
God reveals Himself even to persons completely isolated and

distant from the revelation which began through the Jews and was completed in Christ and His Church. In this way God begins to communicate His call to all mankind, that they should become sharers in the divine nature.[6]

Certain special created realities, however, carry in themselves meanings which God has set aside for special ecclesial use, and special divine instruction for us. For example water, which carries the natural significance of cleansing, is raised to sacred use in Baptism where the cleansing to be effected is spiritual. Bread, of course, carries the natural significance of nourishment. In the Eucharist, bread is raised to sacred use where the nourishment to be effected is spiritual, and so on.

Specific and special created realities are given as sacraments to the Church. The Eastern Churches refer to the sacraments as "the holy mysteries," following the original and scriptural Greek word *mysterion*. In the Roman Church, this concept was translated from the Greek into Latin by two terms: *mysterium* and *sacramentum*. Later in Church history, these two words were used to emphasize two different aspects of the *mysterion*, its interior and its exterior aspects, so to speak. That is, the Latin *sacramentum* came to emphasize the exterior, the visible sign of the mystery, and the Latin term *mysterium*, that interior and hidden reality of salvation.

A sacrament, as the term is used by the Church, has then both an outer and an interior character, both a material and a supernatural part.[7] Yet in all cases, the inner mystery is entirely appropriate to the outward visible part, and consistent with the natural significance it carries from its Creator. These consistent meanings, both the spiritual meanings "naturally" carried in all creation, and the supernatural meanings of sacraments properly so called, are appropriate and fitting and consistent because all creation is of the one God: "for in Him all things were created, in heaven and on earth, visible and invisible, whether thrones or dominions or principalities or powers — all things were created through Him and for Him" (Col 1:16).

Christ Our Sacrament

In the *Catechism*, the Church teaches that in the full sense of sacrament, Christ is the *mysterion*, the Sacrament of God. Specifically, "The saving work of His holy and sanctifying humanity is the sacrament of salvation, which is revealed and active in the Church's sacraments."[8] Each of the seven sacraments of the Church then communicates an aspect of His saving work; each is an encounter with His sanctifying humanity. A sacrament is more than a mere symbol or a representation, because that which is symbolized and that which is re-presented is in truth *present*.

In the sacraments we encounter Christ, not as some vague disembodied spirit but in His resurrected humanity. In Baptism we are incorporated into Christ: we enter into Him, in His Body, in His Church. In Confirmation we meet Christ who strengthens us, not as a concept, not merely in symbol, but as a man fully human and fully God. In the Holy Eucharist it is Christ who comes to us: body, blood, soul, and divinity. In Reconciliation we meet the real and merciful Christ, forgiving our real and human failures. In the Anointing it is the Healer, Jesus Christ, who touches us. In Matrimony it is Christ formed in our human covenant who unites us; in Holy Orders it is Christ our High Priest who sets us apart for His sacred service. These seven sacraments of the Church are all participations in His saving work, and hence we say there are seven sacraments in the Church which itself is like a sacrament, the extension of the saving humanity of Christ at work in time and upon the earth.

We are most concerned with sacraments from the perspective of the New Covenant, but sacraments are prefigured in the Old. The chosen people received signs and symbols from God that distinctively marked their liturgical life and were signs of their covenant with God. Thus for example circumcision (Gn 17:10 ff.), the anointing and consecrating of kings and priests (cf. Ex 28:41), the laying on of hands (cf. Nb 8:10), sacrifices (cf. Lv 3 ff.), and perhaps most importantly the Passover (Ex 12) are seen to prefigure the sacraments of the Church.[9]

It can be seen that each of the sacraments of the New Covenant is for us an efficacious *covenantal* encounter with the Word of God, wherein is our salvation. The seven sacraments not only present Christ to us in our journey of faith, they also recall to us the covenantal history of salvation revealed in the Old Testament. Baptism is seen in type in the ancient Flood, and is our incorporation into Christ for salvation even as Noah and his family found salvation within the ark. Confirmation, a completing and a strengthening of that incorporation unto the spiritual battle of Christian life, can be seen in covenantal type in David the warrior king. The Anointing of the Sick within the Body of Christ can be seen in covenantal type in the restoration by Ezra of the temple which had been left in ruin. Reconciliation, or the Sacrament of Penance, can be seen in covenantal type in Israel in the Exodus: in the Law, and in the wilderness trials, a picture for her repentance and purgation can be seen. The Sacrament of Marriage, as was said, is seen in the original covenant of Paradise, and a type of Holy Orders can be seen in the covenant with Abram where fatherhood and sonship, the priesthood of sacrifice and obedience, are pictured.

These Old Testament pictures are, of course, all imperfect. They only suggest the fullness seen in the ultimate sacrament of the saving humanity of Jesus Christ. And all the sacraments of the New Testament, sacred as they are, stand in relation to the "Sacrament of sacraments," the Eucharist. The Eucharist re-presents in fact and in truth the saving work of the humanity of Jesus Christ, His very body and blood offered in sacrifice. In partaking of this Sacrament, we partake of *Christ*[10] — body, blood, soul and divinity — and we become incorporated into Him. The Eucharist is both Word and Sacrament, because it is Christ Himself, the Word of God and our salvation. Hence the Church recognizes in the liturgy of the Eucharist the very source and summit of the Christian life.

The Church has explained the nature of a sacrament as both sign and instrument of communion with God and of unity among all men.[11] Certainly the saving work of Jesus in His earthly ministry fulfills this definition! Certainly the Church He founded and left to carry on His saving work does, as well. Hence also the Church in Christ, as His Body alive in His Spirit, is a sacrament. As mediator of the sacraments in His name, she is a sacrament: "The Church, then, both contains and communicates the invisible grace she signifies. It is in this analogical sense, that the Church is called a 'sacrament'."[12]

The highest act of God in His self-expression in creation, which was to complete His will to share His divine nature with persons, came in the Incarnation of the Son. God became man: "the Word became flesh, and dwelt among us" (Jn 1:14). "For in Christ the fullness of divinity dwells in bodily form" (Col 2:9). Christ is the most perfect "sacrament," being both the highest material reality, man, and the highest supernatural reality, God Himself. As Schmaus wrote, "The man Jesus Christ is the locus and the means of God's encounter with man. Thus we can call Him the original sacrament."[13] Christ is the perfect self-communication of God to human persons, and the perfect "way" for a human person to achieve his divine destiny of fellowship with God. As Jesus said, "I am the way, and the truth, and the life; no one comes to the Father except through Me" (Jn 14:6).

When Jesus ascended to the Father He left the sacramental ministry of the work of salvation to His Church. The Church, as His Body on earth, was to provide mankind the way to God. That is, the Church, in Christ, was to be "the nature of sacrament — a sign and instrument, that is of communion with God and of unity among all men."[14] Hence now the Church is, even more explicitly, "the universal sacrament of salvation."[15]

The Church can be seen in two ways: as the gathered community of salvation in Jesus Christ, and also as the instrument of that salvation for the world. In carrying out the mandate given her by Christ, she uses the graces and the means of grace provided through the abiding Spirit. The Sacrament, the Church, then provides sacraments, the seven, that all humanity might have saving access in Christ to God.

Incorporation into Christ: Baptism

Baptism is the first sacrament received in the Church. Our concern in this chapter is the importance of this sacrament to the Christian life, and the place it has for us in our journey to holiness. It is essential that we understand the true meaning of Baptism, because the grace and transformation of Baptism become foundational for our whole Christian life. A difficulty arises because of the time in one's life at which Baptism is received. In the Eastern Churches the three sacraments of initiation (Baptism, Confirmation, and Eucharist) are all received at the same time, even in infancy. In the West, adults entering the Church receive the three sacraments of initiation all at the Easter Vigil Mass, on Holy Saturday. For the children of the Church, however, the sacraments are received at different times in their growth, but Baptism is usually administered in their infancy. Baptism is the beginning of our life in Christ!

Because of these variations in when Baptism is received, as well as other reasons, we have in the Catholic Church adults of a wide range of ages and experiences who are all beginners, in the purgative stage of their spiritual journey. There are those who have just been baptized, having recently entered the Church as adults. There are those who were baptized as infants, and remained faithful for perhaps many years in Catholic outward practices, but who have developed spiritually very little since their childhood. There are also those who were baptized as infants, who dropped away from the Church for one reason or another, and who are now developing an attitude of seriousness about their relationship with Christ. All these adults can be beginners in the spiritual journey, alongside a seven-year-old child who has just come into the age of reason, in preparation for the First Sacraments of Penance and Eucharist!

Our God is kind and merciful, and very patient with us. A beginner of advanced years with true yearning for God can make rapid progress. It is important for such an adult to realize the great power in the sacraments, beginning with the sacrament of Baptism. We must understand the supreme dignity of the grace and the virtues we have received in the sacrament, so that we might return to and remain in that grace forevermore. Whether we have just come into God's grace, or just returned to it after many years, or whether we have presumptuously ignored it and taken it for granted until now, *now* we must begin earnestly to respond to our vocation.

Baptism is a word taken from the Greek, meaning to dip, plunge, or immerse. Much of the theology of Baptism is developed in Scripture. Although not explicitly using the word "Baptism," the Church understands Jesus to be speaking of this sacrament when He told Nicodemus of the necessity of the new birth, from above: "Amen, amen, I say to you, unless you are born of water and the Spirit, you cannot enter into the kingdom of God" (Jn 3:5).

In an appearance after His resurrection, Jesus explicitly related Baptism and salvation: "Whoever believes and is baptized will be saved; but whoever does not believe will be condemned" (Mk 16:16). Today the Church continues to believe that Baptism is necessary for salvation, for those to whom the Gospel has been proclaimed and who have had the possibility of asking for the sacrament.[16] After the resurrection, the Church received the very clear mandate to baptize:

> Go, therefore, and make disciples of all nations, baptizing them in the name of the Father and of the Son and of the Holy Spirit, teaching them to observe all that I have commanded you; and behold, I will be with you always, until the end of the age.
>
> Mt 28:19-20

What role does this sacrament have in our spiritual journey? The apostle Paul taught beautifully that Baptism is the beginning of the Christian life, and is in fact our entrance into the saving humanity of Christ:

> Do you not know that those of us who were baptized into Christ Jesus were baptized into His death? Therefore, we were buried with Him through our baptism into death, so that just as Christ was raised from the dead by the Father's glory, we too might be able to lead a new life. For if in baptism we have become sharers in a death like His, we will also share in a resurrection like His.
>
> We know that our old self was crucified with Him in order to do away with the sinful self so that we

might no longer be slaves to sin, for a person who has died is set free from sin.

But if we have died with Christ, we believe that we shall also come to life with Him, for we know that Christ rose from the dead and will never die again; death no longer has any power over Him. For the death he died He died to sin, once and for all, but the life He lives He lives for God. Thus, you too should consider yourselves dead to sin and living for God in Christ Jesus.   Rm 6:3-11

This very significant passage is quoted here in its entirety to stress the mystery of our union with Christ in the sacrament. To be baptized into His death as well as His resurrection reveals to us the call of discipleship even into His death, and the supreme dignity of our union with the glorified Lord.[17] Our Christian journey to holiness and to relationship with God in Christ begins with this rebirth in Baptism to a whole new personal spiritual reality. We enter into His life, and we enter into His death. We enter His redemption not "merely" as recipients of it, but as united with Him in the bringing of it to the world. We are as united with Him in His vocation, as a faithful spouse is to her Husband.

Baptism was linked to the new life in Christ very early in the history of the Church, beginning with the first preaching of Peter following Pentecost. "And Peter said to them, 'Each of you must repent and be baptized in the name of Jesus Christ for the forgiveness of your sins; and you shall receive the gift of the Holy Spirit'" (Ac 2:38). The results of Peter's sermon were abundant:

Those who accepted his word and were baptized — that day about three thousand were won over — devoted themselves to the teaching of the apostles and

to the fellowship, to the breaking of the bread and to
the prayers.   Ac 2:41-42

Similar records are presented in Acts 19:5 and Acts 22:16.

The baptized, Paul teaches, have "put on Christ" (Gal
3:27). The Church holds as it always has, that "Through the
Holy Spirit, Baptism is a bath that purifies, justifies, and
sanctifies."[18] Entry into Christ through Baptism results in what
Paul teaches is a new creation, which accomplishes what was
given in type in the Old Covenant, namely the sign of circumcision: "Neither circumcision nor uncircumcision is of any
significance — a new creation is all that matters. May peace
and mercy be upon all who follow this rule, and upon the Israel
of God" (Gal 6:15-16). In the New Covenant there is a change
in sign and sacrament, corresponding to a change in spiritual
relationship, but not a "change" in God: our God is the same as
the God of Israel.

This "new creation" through faith and Baptism accomplishes the gathering of human persons into the divine life, into
Christ, and so into the life of the Trinity. Peter teaches very
beautifully that this gathering is the fulfillment of the ancient
promise of God:

> May grace and peace abound to you through the
> knowledge of God and of Jesus our Lord. His divine
> power has bestowed on us everything that pertains
> to life and godliness through our knowledge of the
> One Who called us by His own glory and power.
> Through His glory and power He has bestowed on
> us the great and precious promises, so that through
> them you may escape from the corruption that pas-
> sion brought into the world and come to share in the
> divine nature.   2 P 1:2- 4

Baptism gathers us into the life of the Trinity, but not as separated individuals. We are gathered as well into the community life of the Church.[19] Thus we understand the teaching of Paul, "by one Spirit we were all baptized into one body" (1 Cor 12:13). We are bound with one another: "we are members one of another" (Eph 4:25). This gathering into the Church is described by Peter using the image of "living stones," "built into a spiritual house, to be a holy priesthood" (1 P 2:5). This house of God is understood to be the fulfillment of God's ancient promise to David, in establishing His covenant with him and his lineage (2 S 7). This "holy priesthood" of the Church is the fulfillment of God's promise to Moses, in the sacred covenant with him on Mt. Sinai (Ex 19:6).

With this rich scriptural foundation, the Church teaches the spiritual changes brought about in a human person through the sacramental graces of Baptism:

> The fruit of Baptism, or baptismal grace, is a rich reality that includes forgiveness of original sin and all personal sins, birth into the new life by which man becomes an adoptive son of the Father, a member of Christ and a temple of the Holy Spirit. By this very fact the person baptized is incorporated into the Church, the Body of Christ, and made a sharer in the priesthood of Christ.[20]

Through Baptism several crucial changes occur in human persons. These are spiritual realities: no, they are not material visible changes; yes, they are actual, real, and absolutely important. We are cleansed of all sin, and brought into Christ. We are infused with sanctifying grace, and with the theological virtues of faith, and hope, and charity. Following Baptism, there is nothing in the person that God hates. Were a person to die in baptismal grace, he would be immediately gathered into the fellowship of the Holy Trinity, in the beatific vision with God. Thus we see the great dignity and power of Baptism.

Christ Exhorts Us: Remain in Me!

"Abide in Me, and I will abide in you. Just as the branch cannot bear fruit on its own unless it remains on the vine, so neither can you unless you abide in Me" (Jn 15:4). Our call to follow Christ, our destiny in fact to finish His work, requires that we remain in Him. If we fall away from Him, as is possible, we must return, and returning, then remain.

Having entered Christ by Baptism, our spiritual journey is begun. We enter Christian life at Baptism as beginners, in what Catholic tradition calls the purgative stage. Because Baptism does not remove the inclination to sin — concupiscence, which "stems from the disobedience of the first sin" — we commonly fall very early into actual personal sins. This first stage, that of the beginner in spiritual development, needs most to be concerned with the removal of obvious and deliberate sins, most importantly all mortal sins. Sacramentally, this directs our attention to Confession, also called Reconciliation or Penance. This sacrament remains important throughout the spiritual life.

Western society, in which we and our Church in America are immersed today, suffers from a blindness to the holy and a blindness to sin. We whose minds have been more or less formed in this materialistic culture must strive to re-form and re-educate ourselves to see clearly the spiritual realities of life. Sin is a real human possibility, and sin has real spiritual consequences in a human soul. To understand clearly the importance of the Sacrament of Reconciliation in the spiritual journey, we must understand clearly the effects of sin upon us.

Sin in a Baptized Believer

Mortal sin is called mortal because it results in death to the soul. Mortal sin causes the loss of sanctifying grace in the soul, thereby breaking our fellowship with God. Mortal sin causes the complete loss of the supernatural and theological virtue of charity in the soul, thereby leaving us empty of any share in the life of God. For this reason mortal sin is truly sin "to the death" (1 Jn 5:16), resulting in a soul dead to God and to His eternal life. Mortal sin is truly a dreadful spiritual possibility!

Mortal sin eliminates charity in the soul, leaving a person dead to the life of God, but it does not necessarily eliminate either supernatural faith or supernatural hope, unless one sins specifically against these virtues. For this reason, a person in mortal sin can still have faith in a God of forgiveness, and can still personally hope for his own salvation. Such a soul is, however, in the most dangerous of spiritual situations, and is in the most dire need of the grace and forgiveness available to him in the Sacrament of Reconciliation. Without restoration to the life of God in Christ, such a soul stands in the judgment of hell.

Mortal sin is not easy to commit. It is not a trivial choice for a Christian to turn so radically away from his salvation, but it is certainly possible. God wants our love, but love must be freely given to be real love. The freedom to give love necessarily brings also the freedom to refuse to give love, hence mortal sin is a possible choice for us.

For a sin to be mortal, the Church teaches, three conditions are required. The matter involved must be grave, the person must know the seriousness of the offense, and the person must give free consent of his will to the act.[21] What is "grave matter"? The Church points to the Ten Commandments as stating the express will of God, and constituting therefore grave moral matter.

Venial sin is sin that is not "to the death," but rather does weaken and lessen both sanctifying grace and charity in the soul. A sin is venial if the matter involved is not grave, or if the culpability of the person is diminished by lack of sufficient knowledge or lack of free consent of the will. Gravity itself may also be lessened by circumstances: theft, which is against the Ten Commandments, for example may be less serious when less valuable goods are taken, or when little objective harm is done in the stealing.

The beginner, in the purgative stage of his spiritual journey, must be actively concerned with the elimination of obvious and especially mortal sin in his life. Our vocation is the perfection of charity in our human living. Mortal sin destroys charity in the soul, and even venial sin weakens and diminishes it: sin is clearly the first enemy we must fight against.

Any person, however "advanced" or experienced in the revelations of Christ, can still fall into sin, even mortal sin. Hence Christians who have advanced beyond the stage of the beginner must still resist temptations to sin; and if they sin, they have need of the Sacrament of Reconciliation. It is another of the mistaken teachings which are circulating in some Protestant churches that "once saved, always saved." This teaching greatly exalts the saving grace of God, but eliminates either the justice of God or the freedom of the saved person. In any event, the belief presumes salvation forever after the initial justification of Christ. The Church cautions us against this belief as in fact the sin of presumption, presuming upon the mercy and grace of God.

A soul who has known the presence of the resurrected Christ, in the prayer of contemplation, in the illuminative stage of the proficients, still has need of the Sacrament of Confession. Venial sin is more likely than mortal in the illuminative stage, however. Although venial sin does not require the sacramental absolution of Confession, as does mortal sin, still the soul is greatly strengthened against future temptations by the sacrament.

Even an advanced soul in the unitive stage of the perfect has reason to seek the grace of Christ in His sacrament of forgiveness. The Church recommends a "devotional confession" even when no sin is consciously known in the soul, for the grace and blessings given by the sacrament. Such a person may set his human flaws and shortcomings at the altar of the confessional, if he has no conscious sin, and wait for the wise counsel often given through the priest by the graces of his Sacrament of Ordination.

The Strengthening in Confirmation

The Church teaches that Baptism, Confirmation, and Eucharist constitute together what are called the sacraments of initiation, and have a unity which must be protected. Although Baptism clearly brings the Holy Spirit into the believer, and incorporates him into Christ and into the Church, yet the Sacrament of Confirmation is necessary to the faithful for the "completion of baptismal grace."[22] Confirmation brings a needed strength of the Spirit to the believer, enabling him to be the kind of witness to the faith that Christ desires and that the lost world needs. Confirmed Christians, "as true witnesses of Christ," are "more strictly obliged to spread and defend the faith by word and deed."[23] It is seen, then, that Confirmation enables a more mature response to our vocation in Christ: it is a sacrament that moves us forward in our spiritual journey.

The Church understands the anointing with chrism in Confirmation as a deeper identification with Christ and His anointed mission. "By this anointing the confirmand receives the mark, the seal, of the Holy Spirit."[24] The seal marks our complete and "total belonging to Christ."[25]

Our Catholic faith affirms then that Confirmation completes and perfects the grace received at Baptism. Baptism gives the Holy Spirit, and incorporates us into Christ and His Church, but

> Confirmation… is the sacrament which gives the Holy Spirit in order to root us more deeply in the divine filiation, incorporate us more firmly into Christ, strengthen our bond with the Church, associate us more closely with her mission, and help us bear witness to the Christian faith in words accompanied by deeds.[26]

At whatever chronological age it is received, and at whatever spiritual stage of development the soul has attained, Confirmation strengthens the person for the fullness of the Christian life. Confirmation fortifies the soul for the purgations of the beginner, for the trials of the dark night of the senses, for the interior purifications of the illuminative stage, and for the deep and mystical purification of the dark night of the spirit. Finally Confirmation prepares the soul for the apostolic life of the perfect, reflecting as it does the graces of Pentecost which enabled the apostles to do all that Christ intended for them.

Abiding in Christ: Holy Eucharist

"He who eats My flesh and drinks My blood abides in Me, and I in him" (Jn 6:56). The holy Eucharist, when first received, completes the initiation into Christ and His Church, with the most intimate communion of human persons with God. The Eucharist is "the source and summit of the Christian life."[27] Jesus identified Himself with the true bread from heaven, in John's Gospel, giving us a most beautiful theology of the cross, and of the sacrament.

> I am the bread of life. Your fathers ate manna in the desert, yet they died. This is the bread that came down from Heaven, so that you can eat of it and not die. I am the living bread that came down from Heaven. Anyone who eats this bread will live forever; the bread that *I* will give for the life of the world is My flesh.   Jn 6:48- 51

We find in Scripture the institution of the sacrament by Jesus in His Last Supper with His disciples, before He was betrayed into the hands of men who sought His death. It is highly significant that this occurred at the time of the Passover feast.[28] In this way Jesus completed and fulfilled one of the most important sacraments of the Old Covenant.

> While they were eating, Jesus took bread, blessed it, broke it, gave it to His disciples and said, "Take and eat it; this is My body." Then He took the cup and after blessing it He gave it to them and said, "Drink from it, all of you, for this is My blood of the covenant which will be poured out for many for the forgiveness of sins."   Mt 26:26-28

Parallel passages exist in Mark's account (Mk 14:22-24), as well as in Luke's (Lk 22:19-20). In the earliest written account, we have Paul's letter to the Corinthians:

> For I received from the Lord what I handed down to
> you, that on the night He was betrayed the Lord Jesus
> took bread and, after blessing it, He broke it and said,
> "This is My body which is for you. Do this in remem-
> brance of Me!" In the same way He took the cup af-
> ter they had eaten and said, "This cup is the new cov-
> enant in My blood. Do this, whenever you drink it, in
> remembrance of Me!" 1 Cor 11:23-25

Paul then draws some crucially important theological implications for his readers:

> Whenever you eat this bread and drink this cup, you
> proclaim the death of the Lord until He comes.
> Therefore, if anyone eats the bread or drinks from
> the cup of the Lord in an unworthy manner he will
> be guilty of profaning the body and blood of the Lord.
> Let each one examine himself, and then eat the bread
> and drink from the cup. 1 Cor 11:26-28

The exhortation to receive the Eucharist only worthily is
most important for beginners to hear and to accept. The virtue
of reverence is essential to the growth of the soul, because reverence is based upon the appropriate fear of the Lord, which is
the beginning of spiritual understanding. "The fear of the Lord
is the beginning of knowledge; fools despise wisdom and instruction" (Pr 1:7).

The Eucharist is the most solemn and yet joyful sacrament, and was referred to by the Church from the beginning
as *the breaking of the bread.* "And so they devoted themselves
to the teaching of the apostles and to the fellowship, to the
breaking of the bread and to the prayers" (Ac 2:42).

> By common consent they continued to meet daily in
> the Temple, and at home they broke bread, sharing
> their food with joy and simplicity of heart, praising
> God and enjoying the good will of all the people. And
> day by day the Lord increased the number of those
> who were being saved.   Ac 2:46-47

The all-important Catholic doctrine of the real presence
of Christ, body and blood, in the sacrament also finds testimony
from the beginning in Scripture. The Church proclaims: "In the
most blessed sacrament of the Eucharist 'the body and blood,
together with the soul and divinity, of our Lord Jesus Christ and,
therefore, the whole Christ is truly, really, and substantially contained.'"[29] Paul clearly understood the reality of the presence
of Christ in the Eucharist as he wrote, "The cup of blessing
which we bless, is it not a participation in the blood of Christ?
The bread which we break, is it not a participation in the body
of Christ?" (1 Cor 10:16).

The Lord Jesus personally experienced the scandal among
men over the truth of this doctrine:

> So the Jews began quarreling among themselves,
> saying, "How can this man give us his flesh to eat?"
> So Jesus said to them, "Amen, amen, I say to you,
> unless you eat the flesh of the Son of Man and drink
> His blood, you do not have life within you; whoever
> feeds on My flesh and drinks My blood has eternal
> life, and I will raise him up on the last day. For My
> flesh is true food, and My blood is true drink. Who-
> ever feeds on My flesh and drinks My blood remains
> in Me, and I in him. Just as the living Father sent Me,
> and I live because of the Father, so, too, whoever
> feeds on Me will live because of Me. *This* is the bread

which came down from Heaven, not such as your fathers ate and died; whoever eats this bread will live for ever." He said these things while teaching in the synagogue in Capernaum.

Many of His disciples who were listening said, "This teaching is hard; who can accept it?" But Jesus, knowing in Himself that His disciples were complaining about this, said to them, "Does this offend you? What if you were to see the Son of Man ascending to where He was before?"   Jn 6:52-62

Jesus did not shrink back from the scandal of this great mystery of His real presence in the Eucharist; nor does the Church. In the mystery of this most intimate communion with human persons, the Son accomplishes that which saving faith and Baptism begin: our incorporation into Him and into His Church. The Eucharist itself is a foretaste of the final end of mankind, in the blessed presence of God, in the marriage supper of the Lamb (Rv 19:9). It is our most Blessed Sacrament.

The Sacrament of Matrimony

Marriage is a sacred relationship, created by God for our happiness and our holiness. Through marriage God would teach us love and fruitfulness in love, and through our fruitfulness God would fill the earth with beloved human persons made in His image and likeness. Sacramental marriage, with its religious dimension fully realized and lived, is uniquely needed in our times. The Church — and even more so the confused secular world — needs the witness and the blessings of sacramental Christian marriages. Married couples need to recognize and draw from the special graces that the sacrament has for them — not only for their sakes, but for the Church and for the world.

The secular culture around us is experiencing the dissolution of the traditional sense of marriage, and is replacing that traditional sense of solemn covenantal bond with an agreement of mere convenience. What once was "until death do you part," is now "as long as love shall last." And because our sense of love also has degenerated, the longevity of either the love or the marriage is doubtful. Marriage commitment has weakened, and love has become very self-centered and self-serving. Hence many people, even within the Church, are experiencing genuine crises in their marriages and in their families. The world, and even the Church, need the radiant light of sacramental marriages.

Most Catholics do marry and therefore receive the sacrament of matrimony. Since we are all called to holiness and the perfection of charity, it follows that most Catholics need to understand the growth to holiness *within the married state.* "In God's plan, all husbands and wives are called in marriage to holiness."[30] The Church has received beautiful wisdom from the Lord concerning this divinely ordained state, wisdom which can help us reach the sanctity God wants for us. The world needs to see holy marriages! People want to know God's love, a real and personal love. Married couples truly become priests of God's love, not only for one another, but for the whole watching world.

Marks of Sacramental Marriage

Marriage "aims at a deeply personal unity, a unity that, beyond union in one flesh, leads to forming one heart and soul; it demands indissolubility and faithfulness in definitive mutual giving; and it is open to fertility."[31] Human love itself calls us to union: the natural desires of the human heart move us toward relationship, toward intimacy, toward oneness. All these desires bear the image of God, of course, and offer to prepare us for the consummation of our call into fellowship with God. In other words, marriage is a preparation for our life in the Trinity. The deepest and most intimate union possible in human experience is sacred because it is so intentional an image of the supernatural. Marriage is a picture of the saving covenantal love of Christ with His Church:

> Husbands, love your wives, just as Christ loved the Church and gave Himself up for her, that He might sanctify her, by cleansing her with the bath of water and the word. In this way He will be able to present the Church to Himself in its glory, having neither stain nor wrinkle or anything of that sort, but instead holy and unblemished.
>
> "For this reason a man shall leave his father and mother and be joined to his wife, and the two shall be one flesh." This is a tremendous mystery. I am applying it to Christ and the Church, but each of you should in the same way love his wife as he loves himself, and the wife should respect her husband.
>   Eph 5:25-27, 31-32

In sacramental marriage, then, the man comes to experience with his wife, profoundly and personally, the love of Christ for His Church. Through his wife he experiences the love of the Church for her Spouse. The woman also, profoundly and personally from her side of the relationship, comes to know Christ and His divine covenant. In the crucible of joys and sorrows, through times of sharing and of solitude, in the mysteries of conjugal self-surrender, in the fruitfulness of their love two human persons grow in wisdom and sanctity.

Marriage, as the foundation and source of the family, also provides an image of the Holy Trinity. "The Christian family is a communion of persons, a sign and image of the communion of the Father and the Son in the Holy Spirit."[32] Through this privileged encounter, through sacramental marriage, a person can glimpse something of the inner nature of God in the Trinity. We meet the loving authority of the Father, and the generous self-giving of the Son. And through the mutual sacred love itself of each for the other, the love that enlightens us to the divine mysteries, we meet the Holy Spirit who is the divine Revealer.[33]

It is within marriage that we meet most intimately *another person*, and become free from the prison and isolation of self-preoccupation. *Another person* is, and is important, and is beautiful, and is willing to share life itself with *me*. This is a most precious discovery, and lesson. In marriage, the real love which is specific and personal, finding expression in a relationship of two, becomes a bridge or open door to all persons. My love for my wife, my love for my husband, somehow enables me to love others. In the grace of the sacrament, my very human love becomes sanctified and enlarged, and transformed into charity.

Sacramental Marriage is Centered in Christ

The *Catechism* teaches that the human communion in which a marriage is to grow "is confirmed, purified, and completed by communion in Jesus Christ, given through the sacrament of Matrimony. It is deepened by lives of the common faith and by the Eucharist received together."[34] This is essential: it is by their unity in Christ that the marriage union is strengthened, is made pure, and is completed. Unity in Christ establishes a rock upon which the human commitment in marriage is made trustworthy and firm.

Nothing can be more important in a sacramental marriage than the lived and mutually acknowledged dependence of each spouse upon Christ as center, both personally and in their marriage. Like Christ, we came into this world not to be served but to serve (Mt 20:28). Husband and wife, our covenant calling is not to merely satiate natural desires but to bless, to edify, to sanctify the other. Christ graces a couple in sacramental marriage that they might "help one another attain holiness in their married life and in welcoming and educating their children."[35]

A Sacramental Marriage Forms a Catholic Home

In a Catholic home, Christ is to be center. Many American Catholics today live in houses which reflect not our Catholic faith but rather secular values and attitudes. The center object of many living or family rooms, for example, is a television set. This center becomes almost an idol king, consuming the time and attention of family members while shaping attitudes in them which are contrary to the truths of the faith. Most television, which is a major teacher of American children and adults, is immodest, immoral, anti-family, atheistic (that is, God may as well not exist in most programming), materialistic, hedonistic, individualistic, brutal, irreverent, and cynically without hope.

Centered by television, preoccupied with material satisfactions, many families are driven to disintegration. Many which have not physically separated are in fact broken into separate pieces, living separate lives. Separate meals replace family meals together; separate careers or jobs force separate schedules which make family time together impossible. Everyone in the family soon has their own cars, their own televisions, their own schedules, their own jobs, their own lives. Such a family is not a family. A family is to be a community of persons: a common-unity whose reason for unity is love, that is, Christ.

For those in the married state, the ordinary path to holiness must include the *Sacrament* of Marriage, and the Catholic home which results. We must reorder our houses to make them into homes. We must re-gather our separated members and reestablish our families. Our center must be Christ.

When Christ is the center of a home, every aspect of the home reflects that center. Every object in the home must be for the Christian good of the family. The schedule of the family must be ordered to the good of the family. We have so much, in our Catholic culture, to help us in the living of authentic family life, so much to help us grow toward holiness. Sacramentals can help us remember who we are and what is our destination: holy water, the crucifix, pictures of Mary and the saints, an icon of the Sacred Heart, and many other blessed objects of the Church.

The Sacrament of Matrimony is ordered to our holiness, and we must cooperate with its graces. We need to pray together, and share Scripture together. We need to grow together in the Faith, for example reading and discussing together the *Catechism.* As a family we must cooperate with grace in order to grow in Christ. We can watch special video programs designed to edify and encourage. We can spend time together, growing in the beautiful shared intimacy of family life. We can attend as family the various liturgies of the Church, and receive the sacraments together. Christ-centered, we can minister to one another and thereby share in His love for each one of us. Christ enlightens any faith community of persons with saving truth: a marriage and a family centered in Christ is indeed a domestic church[36] founded upon the Rock.

Conclusion to the Chapter

Our growth to holiness in Christ, our response to His call to us to "be perfect, as your heavenly Father is perfect" (Mt 5:48) is a spiritual reality for *human persons*. Our redemption came, and comes, not through pure spirit but through *human* body and soul: through the work of the saving humanity of Jesus Christ, completely God, completely man. All of this is to say that our path to holiness, our journey to God, is intended by God to be a sacramental one. As Catholic Christians, this is our heritage and our common understanding.

Baptism and Confirmation complete our translation into Christ: we are no longer "in Adam," in the old man of sin. In this new creation we have entered, we must grow and develop. If we should fall, and lapse back to the darkness we left, we need to be restored. In our weakness, we should not be surprised by our sin, but we should be deeply grieved and repentant. Confession is given to us for our restoration; Eucharist is given to us for our up-building in Christ. In the journey, the most common state of life is marriage, and in the human love in marriage, God gives us a sacramental encounter with His divine love. Hence our Christian life is sacramental.

How do we use this knowledge in order to walk in wisdom? We must remember the truth, and seek to remain in the truth. As we come to understand more clearly the exalted dignity of a baptized Christian, we will guard more zealously our own place in Him. This we must do. We must consciously know that our life is in Him, and only in Him. In a moment we can fall away, out of Him and into dark selfishness and confusion. In the blink of an eye we can discover ourselves acting, talking, wishing as "mere man." This humiliating fact of our humanity is a serious threat for us as beginners, when even mortal sin is not unlikely. As we advance in the spiritual life and gain some stability in Christ, venial sin becomes more likely the danger, but whatever the depths of our weakness, we stand in need of the sacraments to restore us and then to strengthen us. Our resolute intention needs to be to return to Him, to remain in Him. He is our Sacrament: all our sacraments are encounters with Him, Jesus Christ.

As we grow in faith and in the spiritual life, the sacraments will take on an increasingly luminous and sacred nature. All of the sacraments will become more and more transparent to their outwardly hidden divine reality. Baptism, Confirmation, Eucharist, Confession, and Matrimony will all yield to their interior essence who is Christ. We must always seek deeper insight into our sacramental life, because in it we will find Him.

Notes

1   *CCC*, 1134.
2   See the section "Sacrifice and Priesthood," Ch. 7.
3   See the section "The Sacrament for the Suffering," Ch. 8.
4   *CCC*, 1147, cf. Ws 13:1, Rm 1:19 ff., Acts 14:17.
5   *CCC*, 54, from *Dei Verbum*, 3; cf. Jn 1:3 and Rm 1:19-20.
6   *CCC*, 51, from *Dei Verbum*, 2; cf. Eph 1:9, 2:18 and 2 P 1:4.
7   Matthias Joseph Scheeben, *The Mysteries of Christianity* (St. Louis: B. Herder Book Co., 1964), 559.
8   *CCC*, 774.
9   *CCC*, 1150.
10 *CCC*, 1374.
11 *Lumen Gentium*, 1.
12 *CCC*, 774.

[13] Michael Schmaus, *Dogma 5: The Church as Sacrament* (London: Sheed and Ward, 1992), 7.

[14] *Lumen Gentium,* 1.

[15] *Lumen Gentium,* 48.

[16] *CCC,* 1257.

[17] Thomas Worder, editor, *Sacraments in Scripture* (Springfield, IL: Templegate, 1966), 61.

[18] *CCC,* 1227.

[19] Ibid., 1267.

[20] Ibid., 1279.

[21] Ibid., 1857.

[22] Ibid., 1285.

[23] Ibid.

[24] Ibid., 1295.

[25] Ibid., 1296.

[26] Ibid.,1316.

[27] Ibid., 1324; cf. *Lumen Gentium*, 11.

[28] Ibid., 1340.

[29] Ibid., 1374, cf. Council of Trent (1551): DS 1651 in *The Christian Faith*, 7th revised edition, J. Neuner, SJ and J. Dupuis, SJ, eds. (New York: ST PAULS / Alba House, 2001), #1526, p. 621.

[30] John Paul II, Apostolic Exhortation, *Familiaris Consortio* (Nov. 22, 1981), 35.

[31] *CCC,* 1643.

[32] *CCC,* 2205.

[33] *CCC,* 687.

[34] *CCC,* 1644.

[35] *Lumen Gentium,* 11.

[36] *CCC,* 2204.

CHAPTER SEVEN

GROWING IN HOLINESS: THE MASS

THE THREE STAGES IN THE MASS

The Mass Invites Us to Holiness

Our participation in Holy Mass is our highest and most sublime human action: in the Mass our vocation is completed. Such language may seem exaggerated! Many Catholics do not experience such an ultimate moment in the liturgy, nor are most of us conscious of such a personal fulfillment of calling and life in this celebration of our Church. Indeed, a common unconsciousness of real meaning and act in our communal worship is one of the great problems of the Church in our time. Today many Catholics are present for the Holy Mass, but with little understanding of the realities surrounding and inviting them. Whoever would hope and strive for the holiness God intends for us dare not miss the opportunity offered us at Mass.

There is dynamic *movement* in the Mass, as there is movement in our spiritual and physical life. In recognizing the movement within the Mass, and in welcoming that movement within our own souls, we cooperate with a design for growth that is surely built into life itself. We see, in the liturgy of the Mass, three crucial stages of worship which align exactly with the three traditional stages of spiritual growth. These stages of worship are participations in divine movements of the Spirit. These stages correspond to the stages of discipleship through which Jesus gathered and formed those first disciples He called into His life.

The three stages of the Mass can also be seen as stages of our human life as we respond to His call. First the Word of God calls us, and we approach. This Word gathers us to Himself, to His altar of sacrifice and communion. Then is the second stage at the altar, the cross. The altar is not the end, however: His death is not the end. The altar of sacrifice becomes the table of communion. His self-giving becomes our food for life. This third stage, the end from the beginning, is our communion with Him, and our apostolate therefore in Him. There are therefore these three stages of the Mass: the liturgy of the Word, the consecration at the altar, and the communion of the Lord with His people. We will see the correlation of these three stages of the Mass with the traditional three stages of development and life of the soul: the purgative stage, the illuminative stage, and the unitive stage.

The Church recognizes that regular participation in the sacrifice of the Mass is essential. We are explicitly held under obligation to attend Mass on Sundays and certain holy days, by Church precept.[1] Mere outward observance profits us little or nothing, of course, if we fail to receive personally what is set before us, or to enter personally into the sacred mysteries. The liturgy is an invitation, to which we must respond.

The liturgy of the Mass is called Eucharist, meaning thanksgiving. This word reveals a crucial aspect of the act: thanks*giving*. The Mass is essentially a time of giving, and for us a time of both giving personally and receiving the Gift given.

The Mass is the holy sacrifice of Christ, given for us, offered to the Father. And it is, as well, communal meal offered to us to "take and eat." It is, then, not in contradiction that the Mass requires both giving and receiving. We are invited into our personal sharing, into our self-gift also, into participation with Christ in His humanity as He gives without measure, that we might receive in Him a sharing in His life.

We need to seek an ever deepening understanding of all that is offered to us in Holy Mass. We need to strive in all sincerity to be present to Him as He allows Himself to be made present to us in His sacrifice, and in His meal. The Mass has been faithfully represented to and in the Church for almost two thousand years. It is not the responsibility of the Church to make the Mass transparent to us, or even worse, entertainment for us! It is our responsibility to make ourselves present to Christ, as He makes Himself present to us. We are living in a self-centered time, and we must be on guard against the darkness around us. In the Mass, we have the privilege of joining in the light and the love of Christ, that the blessings of God might be yet available to persons still struggling outside of Him.

The holy Mass forms us and builds us up in holiness. In this chapter we will see how the Mass forms us particularly in the three stages of the spiritual life. In each stage of our journey to holiness, the Mass invites us and engages us with the saving work of Christ. The beginner, the proficient and the perfect all receive what each needs of Christ. The spiritual child, adolescent and adult each learn appropriately at His feet.

The liturgy of the Mass invites us to many truths at once. Several realities within the one life of Christ to which we are invited in the Mass, especially stressed in the Church since Vatican II, are:

    1. God created us as *persons*, having both individual uniqueness and need for relationship. We are not made for isola-

tion, nor for mindless group conformity, but for relationship in charity as whole persons. Holiness requires this wholeness.

2. God gathers us as persons to participate and assist together in the celebration of the Mass. Worship is an act of persons in relationship, first with God and then with others because of God. Hence our worship is not as individuals in isolation, but communally and in public. Personal holiness brings blessing and grace to the Church, from each of us to others and from others to each of us.

3. Our gathering as persons, participating and assisting, is manifest in our communal liturgy of both sacrifice and meal. We are called to personally participate in the sacrifice of Christ, and to be nourished in His word and in Holy Communion with His Body and Blood. Indeed sacrifice becomes meal in Christ: "My food is to do the will of Him who sent Me, and to bring His work to completion" (Jn 4:34).

Sacrifice and Priesthood

The third point presented above calls for more attention because of limitations and excesses in our surrounding culture. Holy Mass is both sacrifice and meal, but the aspect of sacrifice can be lost in our culture of self-gratification and consumption, and the aspect of meal can be misunderstood for the same reason. Many Catholics sadly have fallen, in their understanding of the Mass, toward the preoccupations of the secular culture, and as a result have an excessively horizontal perspective of the Mass. The Liturgy of the Word, for some, becomes merely an individual exhortation for personal enrichment or social betterment; the Liturgy of the Eucharist, merely an individual blessing or a human communal meal. The vertical dimension relating both the person and the whole Church upwards toward God is less and less appreciated, in our very individual and consumer-based society. Both the horizontal dimension of authentic brotherhood, and the vertical dimension of divine worship, are necessary to the fullness of the liturgy.

Sacrifice is essential to our understanding of the faith — the religion — that God desires. The altar, which is both altar of sacrifice and table of the Lord, is the center of the Church.[2] The centrality of the altar reveals also the essential role of the priesthood. Sacrifice requires a priesthood: those set aside and especially graced to offer sacrifice at the altar.

Because the altar of the New Covenant is the cross of the Lord Jesus Christ, we see that a priest who serves at the altar is a representative of Christ in a unique way, completely different from the way all other Christians are called to represent Christ, and to be Christ in the world. This unique configuration to Christ is enabled by the grace of the unique sacrament, the Sacrament of Orders. By this configuration, the ordained priest acts *in persona Christi Capitas*, in the person of Christ the Head. The priest is called to make sacrifices for the people, as Christ did, in a graced human participation in His unique and ultimate priesthood. Just as the one sacrifice of Christ is unique, accomplished once for all, yet is re-presented continually in the Mass; so also the one unique priesthood of Christ is made present in the world through the ministerial priesthood.[3] May God bless His Church with priests!

The Threefold Movement in the Mass

We have seen that Christ completed His spiritual transformation in the apostles in three distinct stages. We have seen that this progressive growth and development of spirituality, of Christian life itself, is reflected in the broadly accepted spiritual theology in the Church in the "three ways." It should not be surprising to us, then, that we can discover three movements of spiritual formation in the holy Mass of the Church.

The center of the Mass is the Eucharistic sacrifice, which Vatican II proclaims as "the source and summit of the Christian life."[4] This sacrifice of the Mass, which makes present to us the passion and sacrifice of Christ, places us then in the saving work of Christ alongside, so to speak, the original disciples and apostles. We are made present, in Christ, to His forming and transforming ministry. In this section we will see that this liturgy gathers us into His threefold formation process as He also gathered His first followers in a work of three stages. Holy Mass, in other words, becomes in us a transforming work of God in three movements, His holy work converting and gathering us into Christ.

Mystical and Liturgical Spirituality

The liturgy is by nature public and collective. It is the worship of the whole Church. It is not uncommon, however, to think of spirituality and personal spiritual growth as very individual and even private realities. Some who think in this way will question not only an essential place for the liturgy in the spiritual life of a person, but any place at all. Such individualistic thinkers might even consider gathering for the Mass an obstacle to spiritual growth. If one considers spiritual experiences to be highly personal and individual matters, then one might want to avoid or minimize communal prayers and the Mass. One might prefer solitude, privacy and intimacy with the Lord. In other words, there is a possible conflict between the very

personal nature of relationship with God, and the call of the
Church to public worship in liturgy.

The problem of possible conflict between the two schools
of spirituality, mystical/individual and liturgical, has a history
and has been investigated. One scholar has observed that some
of the greatest spiritual masters in the history of the Church
did not explicitly and fundamentally involve liturgy in their spirituality. He wrote,

> Neither the desert fathers, nor the great Spanish
> mystics, St. Teresa of Avila and St. John of the Cross,
> nor the promoters of 'devotio moderna,' nor Ignatian
> Spirituality, nor the best representative of 'baroque
> piety,' St. Francis de Sales, offer us any practice of
> devotion congenial with liturgical action, or an inte-
> rior life shaped explicitly by it.[5]

This same observation is made in the classic work on liturgy
by Vagaggini. He specifically considers the traditional theology
of the three ways, and its possible compatibility or incompat-
ibility with liturgical worship.[6] He acknowledges the surface
difficulty: "Someone will surely inform us that actually the greatest mystics spoke but little about the liturgy," referring
specifically to St. Teresa and St. John of the Cross.[7] It is true
that in their writings of mystical doctrine they simply have not
explained the place which the liturgy should or should not have.

Other scholars resolve this difficulty by stating that the
sacramental life is presupposed as present in the lives of these
saints. We presume their liturgical life in the same way that we
assume their practice of basic Christian living and virtue, especially charity. Various spiritualities have been categorized in
the Church; for example the spirituality of Benedict has been
called liturgical, due to the importance that he gives to the Opus

Dei (Divine Office of the Hours) in his Rule. The spirituality of St. Ignatius has been called "voluntaristic," that of St. Teresa, "mystical," and that of St. Vincent de Paul, "ascetical." True Christian perfection of charity, one writer observes, requires all these elements in a complete spiritual theology. "Only through them does the grace of God work freely via charity as the indispensable condition for union with God."[8]

Spiritualities promoted by different writers and saints do differ in certain particular forms and emphases, but the liturgy is basic to them all. A liturgical spirituality, that is, one "attuned to the spirit of liturgy and fostered by it is, by its own nature, more objective and should be considered classical, integral and fundamental."[9] Considered in this way the liturgy is foundational to and belongs to the whole Church and all spiritualities within her. All authentic spiritualities within the Church must be liturgical, at least implicitly.

Vagaggini considers this possible conflict among spiritualities in great detail, and concludes not conflict but beautiful catholic diversity.[10] He presents several mystics who did speak plainly and explicitly of the liturgy in their spirituality (Cassian,[11] and the Venerable Marie of the Incarnation[12]). A whole chapter is devoted to the liturgical spirituality of St. Gertrude called the Great,[13] in whom he finds the perfect marriage between liturgical spirituality and mysticism very well expressed. Vagaggini concludes that "the liturgy is capable of being the center of a complete spiritual doctrine... leading one to the highest state of perfection."[14] This is our goal in this chapter, to better understand the power and place of the liturgy of the Mass in our spiritual journey.

Spiritual Perfection and the Mass

The ordinary teaching of the Church asserts the essential link of the liturgy, especially the Mass, with Christian perfection. The International Theological Commission, an authentic voice of the Magisterium of the Church, has considered the relationship of the liturgy to the "deification," that is, the spiritual perfection, of human persons. The ITC describes the Eucharist as "the innermost and most objective presence of the sacrifice of Christ and the ultimate constitutive element in the building up of the Church."[15] The upbuilding of the Church, by the perfecting of her members in the Mass, cannot be in any way contradictory: it is an inner necessity.

Spiritual perfection, the Commission continues, cannot be thought of as anything contrary to the nature of mankind. Just the opposite is true. Spiritual perfection is the proper goal of human persons. The Commission wrote, "deification properly understood can make man perfectly human; deification is the truest and ultimate hominization of man." Considering then the possible conflict of personal spirituality with communal prayer, they continued, "this deification is not communicated to the individual as such but as a member of the Communion of Saints.... The fullness of deification belongs to the beatific vision of the Triune God, which takes the soul into the Communion of Saints."[16] The ITC is here reflecting the Catholic philosophy of the human person, who becomes complete only in true relationship with his Creator.

Dietrich von Hildebrand wrote beautifully of the effect upon the person of the liturgy, realizing that our goal is full transformation into Christ. In our worship in the liturgy, we both act and are acted upon. Participation in the liturgy causes authentic change within the soul: the liturgy actually forms Christ within us. Von Hildebrand wrote,

> The conscious, fully-awakened act of performing the Liturgy imprints upon the soul the Face of Christ. In taking part in the Liturgy, we make our own the fundamental attitudes embodied in it.[17]

Pius XII, in a 1947 encyclical describing the efficacy of the Eucharistic sacrifice and the sacraments (*Mediator Dei*, #26), wrote:

> It should be clear to all, then, that God cannot be honored worthily unless the mind and heart turn to him in quest of the perfect life, and that the worship rendered to God by the Church in union with her divine Head is the most efficacious means of achieving sanctity.

Here the Holy Father made explicit the essential link of the quest of perfection with ecclesial worship. Since the Church most perfectly worships in her union with the sacrifice of Christ in the Mass, we can conclude "the most efficacious means of achieving sanctity" is to be found in personal participation at holy Mass. At Mass, our Christian formation is most truly ordered to Christ Himself, in ways that we will explore in detail later.

The Vatican II teachings on the Eucharist similarly assert its privileged place in the spiritual life of Christians. The Eucharist "is the supreme means whereby the faithful may express in their lives, and manifest to others, the mystery of Christ and the real nature of the true Church."[18] Again (Article 8): "In the earthly liturgy we take part in a foretaste of that heavenly liturgy which is celebrated in the holy city of Jerusalem toward which we journey as pilgrims, where Christ is seated...." And again (Article 10), we read that the liturgy is the high point toward which the many works of the Church are directed, while at the same time the source of her power for those works. The goal and purpose of her apostolate is the gathering of His children into the praise and worship of God, to His Sacrifice, to the Supper of the Lamb. Truly there is a clear voice in the Church for the essential place of the liturgy in our journey toward the perfection of charity.

Stages in the Celebration of the Mass

As we participate in Holy Mass, the Mass is nurturing us and forming us into Christ. In considering the formative effect upon us in the liturgy of the Mass, it is important to realize that in all probability, the congregation consists of several very different groups of souls. Some are beginners, and are struggling to overcome outward and obvious sin. But some may be caught in the trials of purgation, or may sit released from the darkness of a recent cross, perplexed, lost, confused, and afraid about what might come next for them. Some, the proficients in the illuminative stage, may be in a quiet adoration of the resurrected Christ, present and real within them. Some may be in the hidden ecstasy of the perfect, in the unitive stage, rapt in personal union with the Bridegroom of the Church.

The radically different spiritual realities in these stages are instructive to consider, in order that we might better understand the work of the liturgy in the whole Church, and in us personally. "In brief, then, the first stage is to empty oneself of selfishness, with the help of His grace. The second stage is to receive from God, for it is for Him to pour Himself into the soul and take over the direction of the conscience through the predominating action of the gifts of the Holy Spirit."[19] In the third stage, the person has entered the ministry of the Word as an active member of His Body, and without contradiction as a true contemplative, corresponding to apostolic discipleship after Pentecost.

Although the common focus in the liturgy of each person should be Jesus Christ, yet the formation which each needs, differs. The beginners need exhortation in their active struggle against sin. The help of His grace in the Mass and the support of the Church are necessary and even urgent to them, lest they fall to the many temptations which assail them. Those who are the proficients need to be encouraged to a more interior but even stronger faith, to an "active" and faithful submission to His purifying work within the soul. This second group is experiencing passive purgation, with the Holy Spirit as the active one: their essential and interior activity is faithful cooperation with the Spirit. Any members of the third group, the perfect, in the congregation are a source of great graces for the Church. Through their merits and prayers in the communion of saints, even if in quiet worship, they call down the grace and upbuilding of divine power upon their brothers and sisters around them, bringing glory to God in their praise. Their need, in the liturgy, is in truth the grace for personal martyrdom: their part in the Church is to lay down their lives for the Church, as did their Master.

Even though God's work in them is more interior and hidden, it must be said that souls in the illuminative and perfect stages are by no means retired, reclusive (except for special callings), or passive Christians. Just the opposite is the case. "Good works, even monumental ones, become the hallmark of the illuminative way."[20] In *The Soul of the Apostolate*, Dom Chautard asserts that "the effectiveness of the Church's apostolate is directly related to the number of Christians who have entered the illuminative way."[21] Christians in this second stage do works of charity because they want to: it is in their heart to act out the love God has given them. Beginners need exhortation to give, against the selfishness they still struggle with, but the proficient need more encouragement to trust in the love they have indeed begun to know. All need the graces poured out to His Church in Holy Mass.

Contemplation

More has been said in the earlier chapter on prayer about the stages of prayer which accompany the stages of spiritual growth. We saw how the two are most intimately connected. To understand the movements of the liturgy relative to the stages of spiritual growth, it is necessary to know, specifically, the radical change in prayer communication with God which occurs when a soul enters the illuminative way. The illuminative way is identified with the beginnings of the prayer of infused contemplation. The way of the perfect is marked by a habitual remaining in contemplation before God. This experience of contemplation is an immediate (that is, non-mediated) awareness of the presence of God very near to or even within the soul.

In no sense is true contemplation a retreat or escape from the apostolic mandate which was given to the Church.[22] Contemplation brings an attitude of openness to God, with a stance of humble obedience to God's word. A contemplative is most deeply a hearer and a servant of the divine word. Von Balthasar expresses this unity of hearing and doing:

Contemplation has to be conceived of biblically; then it includes the total answer of the faithful man to

God's word: which is unconditional devotion to this word and to its purpose of world redemption.[23]

Biblical examples of contemplative response to the call of God include Moses, "who lifted up his arms to heaven during the battle and, despite his position on the mountain, in this way fought alongside the people of God as they struggled below," as Origen emphasized. In this way of contemplation Anthony, father of the monastic life, fought his active spiritual war against evil out in the desert. In this way Teresa of Avila sought reform in the Carmelites, that by true contemplative prayer there would be renewal in the Church following the losses of the Reformation. Through contemplation Thérèse of Lisieux sought to empower missionary expansion, meriting her declaration by the Church as patron of missions. Charles de Foucauld prayed before the tabernacle in the desert daily, "knowing he could not help the world more deeply in any other way."[24]

Contemplatives, who are those Christians in the illuminative and the unitive ways, are profoundly responsive to the word of God. They may be called to solitude in a hermitage, or they may be called to public martyrdom, but they are being called by God and they know it. This characteristic of contemplation is more than personal. It will be reflected in the movement of our public prayer, the liturgy of the Mass.

Movements of the Spirit in the Mass

The liturgy of the Mass can be seen in three parts, three transforming movements of the Spirit within the Church. These are three movements of embrace by Christ toward His Bride the Church, reaching out to her, so to speak, to gather her fully and completely *as she is* toward Himself. Each part or stage of the Mass is particularly effective to its corresponding stage in the spiritual development of the soul: the first movement of the Mass speaks especially to the beginners on the spiritual journey; the intermediate movement, to the intermediate stage in the soul; the final movement, to the final destiny of every soul — intimate communion with her Lord.

The First Movement of the Mass and the Purgative Stage of the Soul

The first movement of the Mass includes the following three parts: the gathering of the people, the Liturgy of the Word, and the Offertory. All of these in this first movement of the Spirit at work in His people speak especially among and to and for those beginners in the Church who are in the purgative stage, whose work is their own gathering, return, purgation, offering.

1. The Gathering of the People

Liturgy as a public work is an innovation in the conversion of an individual. The gathering itself, into Church, is important and significant. Beginners in the spiritual journey, whose concern is predominantly the struggle against sin and the conversion to God in Christ, are not far from the isolation and apparent independence of individualism. Apart from the demands of God, we were "free" from the demands of community. We were autonomous, or so it seemed. We could choose to go here or there, to prefer this or that, to join or remain alone. But conversion to God in Christ brings certain demands, outside of our own choosing. Now I am under obligation to Christ, and to Christ in His Church. Now attendance among His people is no longer my own option, so to speak, but a requirement laid upon me. They have obliged me to be here, with them, and so in the gathering itself my own personal sacrifice begins.

The sacrifice of self is not a negative, of course. There are ways to positively describe what is happening: we are family, and we want to gather as family; we are needy, and we want to meet at our source of graces; and so on. Yet the essential *giving over* that is intrinsic to the gathering should not be overlooked or understated. Our *life* in Christ, that is our share in the everlasting and divine life of our calling, is of necessity and by nature bound up with sacrifice, with self-giving, with preference for the other, with the kenosis of Christ. The cross of Christ is inseparable from our salvation and our vocation: not only the cross that Jesus took up, but the cross that we must take up if we want to follow Him. There are not two crosses: His cross remains, His sacrifice mysteriously remains and awaits completion in His Body, His Church. The gathering into Church, as we await the Mass, is the beginning of the sacrifice and part of the sacrifice. In Christ we are not free to abstain or remain alone! We are free to leave Him! But if we choose to remain in Him by God's grace, we are committed to follow Him in His sacrifice for others.

In our gathering, we look around and see others for whom Christ died and others for whom we are invited to sacrifice also. In gathering we see the invitation into Christ more clearly, and we understand more clearly that in Him we are not and cannot ever again be alone. In sin, outside of Christ, we had the dubious freedom of autonomy and the illusion of independence. As Jesus told Peter, "When you were young, you fastened your belt and went where you wanted" (Jn 21:18). In gathering, under obedience to Christ in His Church, we offer sacrifice. We place that "freedom" at His feet, and offer ourselves *with the Church* to His rightful worship.

2. The Liturgy of the Word

The Liturgy of the Word, including as it does the penitential rite, the readings from Scripture, and the homily, is especially important and significant to the beginner in the purgative stage of the spiritual journey. The purgative stage is especially concerned with purgation, with repentance, with conversion and commitment to Christ. Acknowledgment of sin in the penitential rite is immediately necessary to the beginner, only now turning or recently returning from serious alienation from the ways of God. Very near to spiritual death is the beginner, in the sense that he is so recently taken out of mortal sin. Sin for the beginner is most usually synonymous with mortal sin, and its reality and threat should be very clear in his consciousness. The penitential rite is food itself for the beginner, strengthening him as it does in the personal reality of repentance, the prayers of the Church and the mercy of God.

In the readings of Scripture, and in the homily of the liturgy the beginner is especially formed and fortified. In this movement of transformation the Spirit is making disciples of Jesus Christ. Here the minds of the young in Christ are being taught and enlightened in His radically different and life-changing ways. Here the light of truth is revealed and cast into the thoughts, memory and reasoning of the disciple in formation, illuminating that mind with the mind of Christ. The salvation story of the house of Israel, the revelations of Christ, the work of the Spirit among the apostles — all of Scripture, inspired by God and empowered to do His work, embraces the beginner in the transforming movements of the purgative stage. Here is the Word coming alive among His people again:

> For the word of God is living and active, sharper than
> any two-edged sword. It pierces to the dividing line

between soul and spirit, joints and marrow, and it can discern the innermost thoughts and intentions of the heart.   Heb 4:12

It is not that only beginners need the penitential rite, or the exhortations of the Word, of course. The whole Church needs the whole liturgy of the Mass, but differently. Beginners have immediate personal need in their unique struggles, and so have a special right to this part of the Mass done well. Pastors in their care for the souls entrusted to them can see the many needs of the congregation. How urgent are the needs of these beginners! How precarious is their position, how dangerous their situation! They need the guidance of the Church to help them turn away from the temptations of sin, and to embrace rather the ways of Christ! They need the truth to be set before them, and explained. They need to have the errors of the world exposed. They need to have the confusions of false teachings unveiled and laid bare. They need to be encouraged and exhorted to walk bravely in the path of salvation. The Liturgy of the Word is ordered to all this and more.

There are disturbing divisions in the Church today, and beginners are especially vulnerable to the work of the enemy of souls in these divisions. Contentions confuse the beginner: he barely knows the ways of truth, and hardly understands the revelations of God. Beginners are especially endangered by the false teachers and false shepherds that Jesus warned of even within the Church. Pastors of souls then have special responsibility to feed these sheep, and to protect them from the thieves that sneak in to steal, to kill, and to destroy, even the wolves disguised as sheep. Our Church today is in critical need of clear teaching, of trustworthy teachers, of authentic doctrine. Beginners, analogous to children in natural human development, are uniquely sensitive to the effects of early formation, and they are

in serious danger if the household of their upbringing is per-
verted in some way. The Liturgy of the Word is specifically
"teaching time," and immediately *formative time*, for beginners
in the purgative stage of their spiritual development.

3. The Offertory

The offertory rite also is a part of the sacrifice of the Mass
that is uniquely significant to the beginner. In the offertory, the
creation itself is offered back to the Creator in the form of the
bread and wine, and in the financial offerings of the congregation as tokens of the congregation itself. The priestly offering
to the Father of all creation is part of the vocation of the whole
Church, and is particularly a part of the lay apostolate shared
by most beginners. This offering of all is personal also: it is an
offering of self in the way of all that I have, and work with, and
influence. It is an offering of all creation to become Christ, in a
sense, in the bread and wine: that the whole creation might enter His dominion and reign and incarnation. Just as the whole
creation fell in the sin of Adam, and has been "groaning" (Rm
8:12) until now, so all are called into renewal in Christ. When
the gifts are brought to the altar in the offertory, the beginner
is invited to see himself as well there on the altar, again at the
crossroads of conversion and choice. It is the time of renewal
and commitment, of self offering and prayer for enabling
strength.

The offertory is a crossroads of conversion and choice for
the beginner, in a way parallel for the apostles to the events immediately preceding the passion and cross of Christ. In the
Mass, these are the rites leading soon to the holy sacrifice itself, to the re-presentation of the sacrifice of Jesus Christ in the
hands of the priest. These were times of foreshadowing and pre-
dictions hardly understood by the apostles. These were the

events just before the shameful denials, when they all deserted Him and ran in fear. The offertory is an event of crisis and decision for the beginner. It is an invitation to His altar, with all that this means. The banquet table is being set, but on the other side of a cross! "You prepare a table before me in the presence of my foes" (Ps 23:5).

The correspondence, and appropriateness, of the Liturgy of the Word with the purgative stage of the spiritual journey is grounded in the convicting and convincing power of the Word of God. It is "by hearing the message of salvation the whole world may believe, by believing it may hope, and by hoping it may love."[25] The fundamental nature of the Liturgy of the Word in the life of all Christians was asserted at Vatican II:

> In the sacred books the Father who is in heaven comes lovingly to meet his children, and talks with them. And such is the force and power of the Word of God that it can serve the Church as her support and vigor, and the children of the Church as strength for their faith, food for the soul, and a pure and lasting fount of spiritual life. Scripture verifies in the most perfect way the words: "The Word of God is living and active" (Heb 4:12), and "is able to build you up and to give you the inheritance among all those who are sanctified" (Ac 20:32; cf. 1 Th 2:13).[26]

Such transforming power is certainly not limited to those who are beginners! All Christians are blessed and formed in the Liturgy of the Word. For beginners, however, this part of the Mass is nurturing milk: "Like newborn babes, long for the pure spiritual milk, so that through it you may grow up to salvation" (1 P 2:2).

The Second Movement of the Mass and the Illuminative Stage of the Soul

The second movement of the Mass includes the anaphora: the Eucharistic prayer, "the heart and summit of the celebration."[27] In this prayer are several parts: the preface, the epiclesis, the institutional narrative, and the anamnesis.

1. The Preface

In the Preface are opening prayers gathering the whole community, prayers of thanksgiving and praise, a joining with that unending praise of the Church in heaven with all the angels and saints. For a soul having entered the illuminative stage of the spiritual journey, this sense of unity with the whole Church is especially real and potent. A proficient has received an experiential reality, of standing with Mary and John at the foot of the cross, and hearing in a life-transforming way the words "Behold your mother," "Behold your son" (Jn 19:26-27). For this soul the Church has entered his heart, and she has been taken "into his own." We are one with the angels and saints, and our worship is one. This is a most personal communion, and this prayer is most real. The proficient, then, is especially present with the priest in this prayer, and the whole Church is gathered with them.

2. The Epiclesis

In the celebration of the Mass the Epiclesis ("invocation") is a prayer of appeal, set before God, asking the Father to send the Holy Spirit, the Sanctifier, so that the offerings may become the body and blood of Christ. In the Epiclesis of the Mass, the material substances of bread and wine wait on the altar for a gathering into divine reality, which only God can do. Humanity must wait for God to act. The whole Church waits, in anticipation in this prayer, for this supernatural event. The experience of waiting in human emptiness is uniquely familiar to the soul having recently entered the stage of the proficients: illumination comes to the soul usually following the emptiness of a dark night of the senses. This dark night, as we have seen, precedes the illuminative stage just as the apostles' experience with the dark night of the cross preceded their illumination with the resurrected Christ. In the Epiclesis of the Mass, we appeal to God out of a world of death, in barrenness and poverty; God answers with divine and transforming love.

3. The Institutional Narrative

In this part of the prayer, "the power of the words and the action of Christ, and the power of the Holy Spirit, make sacramentally present under the species of bread and wine Christ's body and blood, his sacrifice offered on the cross once for all" (CCC, 1353). The presence of Christ is now upon the altar, real and entire. The reality of His presence, a supernatural reality scorned by unbelievers but held to faithfully by the Church, is uniquely grasped and loved by the soul having entered the illuminative stage. The presence of Christ in the Sacrament is invisible to the natural eye and absurd to the natural mind unaided by grace, but it is recognized in an immediate and unexplainable way by the proficient. For this soul, the presence of Christ now on the altar is as real and definite as He was to the apostles in the Upper Room following His resurrection: the two appearances are in a sense interchangeable. For souls in the illuminative stage present at the Eucharistic prayer, and for the souls present in the Upper Room, *Christ is now here in glory.*

In this second movement of the Mass, the Holy Spirit is

working the transformation of the Church into glory. "So all of us who gaze with uncovered faces at the glory of the Lord are being transformed into His image, from one level of glory to the next; and this comes from the Lord, who is the Spirit" (2 Cor 3:18). The apostles beheld this glory, resurrection glory, during that stage of their formation that Christ worked in them during the forty days. In this stage of their formation, and in the illuminative stage of souls today, the Spirit is lifting up the Church to glory. In the illuminative stage inner light is received into the soul, which leads her to love God not merely in striving to flee sin, which was the dominant concern of the purgative stage. In the illuminative stage, the soul is moved to a higher and purer virtue, "by imitating the virtues of Christ, His humility, meekness, patience...."[28] Entrance into this stage of the spiritual journey begins a radically different relationship with God, that radically deepens one's participation in the Mass. Now knowing the experiential presence of Christ in contemplative prayer, the sacramental presence of Christ at Mass is also personally and immediately *real*.

4. The Anamnesis

In the Anamnesis ("remembrance"), the Church calls to mind the passion, resurrection, and glorious return of Christ, and presents His offering to the Father which reconciles us with Him. Only because of the reconciliation He won for us can we dare approach the altar for the consummation of the Mass in Holy Communion. Only "through Him, with Him, in Him, in the unity of the Holy Spirit" is the communion of the Church in Christ possible. In this prayer, the souls in the illuminative stage know the pains of disunity experientially, personally. In union with the priest they pray for the union which the coming conclusion to the Mass will signify and cause. They know their own imperfections most sharply, and those they do not know within themselves they fear and hate most of all. These imperfections and sins, venial though they may be, hurt the Church and their Lord, and wound the communion He wants. Here the proficients hunger deeply for the blessed food about to come, yet mourn within themselves over their own sins and the sins of the world, that impede the full communion of the Lord.

The Climax of the Mass — Communion — the Final Vocation of the Soul

The third transforming movement of the Spirit in the liturgy of the Mass brings about the communion of the Body of Christ. In the context of the liturgy, it is here that the Church becomes what she is, the Body of Christ, herself a sacrament of communion between God and human persons. Being a sacrament, the Church lives her apostolate in carrying Christ to the world. In carrying Christ out to the world, she follows the model demonstrated by the apostles after Pentecost. This sacramental apostolate, lived in the apostles after Pentecost, sets the pattern for the perfection of charity and the living of the ministry of the Word. Today, this perfection of the Christian life is found in the final stage of development of the soul, the stage of the perfect, of those in the unitive way. That is, the culmination of the Mass, Holy Communion, looks back to apostolic faithfulness, and is directed in the souls of communicants to the perfection of charity within them.

Communion in the Mass is specially ordered and directed toward, in a sense, full maturity of the soul in the unitive stage. Required of the whole Church in this sacrament is free and worthy acceptance of the free gift — this is all we can do in this movement of the liturgy. It is His work, for which His grace and our cooperation have prepared us. He has prepared us in life through our purgations and the obedience enabled by grace, even through dark nights; He has prepared us in the liturgy of the Mass through our movements of repentance and formation in the Word, and our final preparation and prayer of epiclesis. In the transubstantiation of the Eucharistic prayer, when the resurrection glory of Christ becomes present among us on the altar, we again "remember" the forty days. Transformation in the Church by the resurrected Christ is again at work among us, in His glorious presence at Mass.

The awareness of this reality is especially keen to souls in the illuminative and unitive stages of the spiritual journey, and they are present to Him on behalf of the whole Church in a special and priestly way. The whole Church is nourished in the Eucharist, of course, and each soul is graced and grows in worthy reception of Christ. Those souls in the unitive stage of the spiritual life, however, and to a lesser degree those also in the proficient stage, are uniquely ready to offer themselves with Christ upon the altar. Those souls are uniquely present to Him, in communion with Mary and the Beloved Disciple at the foot of the cross in a special and personal way. In the mystery of Christ, it is through His death in love that life is brought forth. His death is life for us: those who have matured in Him stand with Him, bearing their personal cross at the sacrifice. All are called to take up the cross and follow Him: this is understood and received as personal lived reality for the perfect, and to a lesser degree, the proficient.

The Heavenly Liturgy, and Ministry of the Word

The Mass is the visible expression, revelation, and enfleshment on earth of the heavenly reality which is the eternal liturgy. But the Church, in celebrating the liturgy on earth, is not merely symbolizing this heavenly liturgy while separate from it. The Church in her celebration takes part in the heavenly liturgy (CCC, 1139), and demonstrates and enacts her part in the Body of Christ. She becomes His Body more completely. The Mass is our enactment, so to speak, of the Communion of Saints.

The heavenly liturgy is our destiny and goal: to live before God, in worship of him forever. The celebration of the liturgy on earth is a true sign with efficacy: it serves to lead us into the eternal liturgy.[29] The variety of sacraments, which all point to the liturgy of the Mass, show a consistent pedagogy of the Spirit. This divine accommodation of us on our spiritual journey, this condescension on the part of the Spirit, is His divine sharing in the ministry of the Word: the final stage of the re-gathering by the Father who is the Origin of all. These are indeed the last days.

Christian Perfection, Through the Three Stages of the Liturgy

Within this overall movement of grace for the Church is a threefold movement of the Spirit, which has particular and special efficacy in the formation of the soul, according to his stage of discipleship in Christ on the journey. Therefore believers are able to resonate and receive from the Spirit according to their progress along the road. Fr. Jean Corbon[30] notes that indeed for every sacrament of the Church there is:

1. A "Liturgy of the Word" in which the Spirit manifests Christ to the hearers.
2. A transformation in Christ, accomplished by the Spirit, of

the sacrifice. In its prayer of epiclesis which calls out to God, in every sacrament the Church offers to God her sacrifice in union with Christ.

3. The "synergy of communion in which Christ is communicated and which overflows into the lived liturgy."

Fr. Corbon observes these three movements present in all sacraments. These three movements can be seen as parallel to the three stages of the spiritual life, observed in traditional Catholic spirituality. We can therefore speak of three presentations of Christ in the liturgy, one unique to each of the three stages of spiritual life in His Church. We see that each sacrament presents for the Church:

1. An initial movement appropriate to, and formative for, the beginners on the journey. This is presented in the Liturgy of the Word of that sacrament.

2. A movement of transformation. This presentation to the Church is especially significant to those in the illuminative stage, who are — within their own souls — experiencing the Real Presence of the risen Christ, and in prayer encounter Him in infused contemplation.

3. A movement of communion. In this communion, which accomplishes and is union with Christ, the end of mystical spirituality is achieved. This is the reality of the unitive stage, anticipating the beatific vision itself.

These movements of the Spirit, these presentations to the Church revealed in all sacraments, find their summit in the Eucharist, in the liturgy of the Mass. All Christians can receive grace in the liturgy of the Mass, culminating in Holy Communion; those in the unitive stage have lives which cohere with the Blessed Sacrament.

Conclusion to the Chapter

The ordinary path to holiness is a path liturgically celebrated, nourished and completed in the Holy Sacrifice of the Mass. In the Mass, we have the opportunity to present ourselves to the Lord in worship. In our self-offering, we also make ourselves available to Him for His transforming work within us. We become present, in our true worship of Him, to the powerful emanations of God liturgically made present to His Church.

These emanations of God become movements of the Holy Spirit within the receptive soul, working a transformation. What is this transformation? It is what the Fathers of the Church used to speak of as our deification. It is the work of God gathering us into saving relationship with Him. It is the ministry of Jesus Christ, "the pioneer and perfecter of our faith" (Heb 12:2), drawing us closer to the end of our call to holiness and fullness of life in Him.

In the Mass the movements of worship follow the movements of the saving work of Christ on earth. The illuminations of His life in the liturgy today correspond to the transformations within His first followers, revealing the three traditional spiritual stages.

1. In the Liturgy of the Word, we are again made present to the Christ on earth, and we find ourselves walking, as it were, with the original followers of Jesus. With them we are called to repent and believe; with them we are beginners in the spiritual life. Through the power of the Word we are stirred to purify ourselves, and to be faithful as beginners to the purgative stage of spiritual development.
2. In the Anaphora of the Mass, the resurrected Christ becomes present to us on the altar. We find ourselves prostrate, as it were, before Him in the Upper Room. With

Thomas we can only say, "My Lord and my God" (Jn 20:28). We can only wait with the others; we wait upon Him. He and He alone can cause this transformation in us, whereby the resurrected Christ becomes our reality. Through the power of His risen life we are made proficients, and disciples in the illuminative stage of spiritual development.

3. In the Holy Communion of the Mass we enter the most intimate participation in His life. We become His Body; we join Him in the cup of His Blood. His sacrifice becomes our food and our life; His mission becomes ours. Through the power of His saving humanity we are made perfect and apostles and contemplatives in the unitive stage of spiritual development.

Does this happen in the Mass? Are we so transformed? The potential becomes clear to us, as we understand the spiritual journey and the supernatural essence of the Mass. At each Mass, these three movements of the Spirit are released. With every liturgy, the three stages of spiritual development are nourished, fed, fortified, and encouraged. With every Mass the entire Church is built up. Each one of us, in our own personal "yes" to Him, is moved closer to our vocation to holiness in Him.

Our obligation is to be there at Mass, to present ourselves alongside our brothers and sisters, to worship and to be formed by Him. Wave after wave, the Spirit washes upon us, in His threefold illumination of divine life, inviting us to purity, to holiness, to perfection.

Notes

1. *CCC*, 2042-43.
2. Ibid., 1182.
3. Ibid., 1545.
4. Vatican II, *Lumen Gentium,* 11.
5. German Martinez, "Sacramental Mystery and Christian Spirituality," *Studies in Formative Spirituality* III, No 3 (Nov. 1982): 389.
6. Cyprian Vagaggini, O.S.B., *Theological Dimensions of the Liturgy,* trans. Leonard J. Doyle and W.A. Jurgens (Collegeville, MN: Liturgical Press, 1976), 650.
7. Ibid., 713.
8. Martinez, 390.
9. Ibid.
10. Vagaggini, 660.
11. Ibid., 717.
12. Ibid., 722.
13. Ibid., 740 ff.
14. Ibid., 738.
15. "The Priestly Ministry," *International Theological Commission: Texts and Documents,* ed. Rev. Michael Sharkey (San Francisco: Ignatius Press, 1989), 62.
16. "Theology, Christology, Anthropology," *ITC: Texts and Documents,* p. 216.
17. Dietrich von Hildebrand, *Liturgy and Personality* (Manchester, NH: Sophia Institute, 1986), 17.
18. Vatican II, *Sacrosanctum Concilium,* 2.
19. A Discalced Carmelite Nun, *The Stages of Prayer,* 3.
20. Benedict J. Groeschel, *Spiritual Passages,* 83.
21. Ibid.
22. It is an imperfect understanding of contemplation which leads to the erroneous belief in a conflict between liturgical and mystical theology, discussed earlier.
23. Hans Urs von Balthasar, *Who is a Christian?* trans. John Cumming (New York: Newman Press, 1967), 77.
24. Ibid.
25. Vatican II, *Dei Verbum,* 1.
26. Ibid., 21.
27. *CCC,* 1352.
28. Garrigou-Lagrange, *Three Ages of the Interior Life,* vol. 1, 70.
29. Jean Corbon, *The Wellspring of Worship,* trans. Matthew O'Connell (New York: Paulist Press, 1988), 84.
30. Ibid., 99.

CHAPTER EIGHT

HOLINESS IN SUFFERING AND DYING

The Ordinary Life of Martyrdom

> Precious in the sight of the Lord
>> is the death of His faithful ones.
> O Lord, I am Your servant,
>> I am Your servant, the son of Your handmaid.
>> You have loosed my bonds.
> To You will I offer sacrifice of thanksgiving,
>> and I will call upon the name of the Lord.
>>> Ps 116:15-17

Living and Dying in Christ

Suffering and death are unavoidable, but they need not be wasted. All that is allowed, is allowed for our good — even the hard experiences. In Christ, a human person can experience *even while suffering* a great visitation of joy: the joy of His goodness, His love, His life.

The Christian life of a human person finds its meaning, its depth, its truth in giving. Ultimately we can fully discover our true selves only in sincere self-gift (*Gaudium et Spes*, 24). Here the great dignity of the human person is seen, here the image of God the Holy Trinity is illuminated for us within our own humanity.

Life calls forth love from us: to have life, we must have love. Love calls forth self-giving from us, but self-giving calls forth our dying! So we confront the mystery: to live, we must die. Praise God for the resurrection of our Lord! Death is not the end, it is the final beginning — and so we walk in hope.

Our life-journey into Christ necessarily brings our personal encounter with death. Death is inescapable, yet in another sense it is overcome in Christ. In one sense a disciple of Christ is free from death, yet in another he is more bound to it than any other person. If I do not daily take up my cross, and hence my death, I am not worthy to be His disciple (Mt 10:38, Lk 9:23). Death is a daily possibility for any person, but dying is a daily opportunity for Christians: the dying of each day is a participation in the passion of our Lord and Brother.

Dying is intimately part of our life-journey to God. We have seen that the journey itself is usefully seen as a development in stages: first in the purgative stage of the beginners, then in the illuminative stage of the proficient, finally in the unitive stage of the perfect. Many spiritual writers, notably St. John of the Cross, observe that each transition to the next higher stage is experienced in a preceding night of darkness. In this dark night God is working in the soul a necessary preparation for the new and more intimate relationship with Him which is approaching.

Stages of Dying

We can see that these nights also form a sequence of stages for the soul in its journey toward and into Christ: three nights are three stages of dying. That is, there are three stages of dying to the old man, as there are three stages of living in the new. There are three stages of dying in Adam, together with the three stages for the soul of living and loving in Christ. There is the first dark night, the night of the senses according to St. John of the Cross; and there is the second dark night, the night of the spirit. The final dark night which the soul experiences in its journey to Christ is the night that we call death itself.

The stages of dying are not to be seen negatively. It is true that death is an enemy, in one sense. It is the last enemy to be destroyed by Christ before the complete revealing of the kingdom (1 Cor 15:26). It is an intrinsic part of the judgment of God upon mankind after the fall in the Garden of Eden. Death was the promised consequence of disobedience (Gn 2:17) which Adam and Eve experienced immediately in their souls, as they fell into mortal sin and separation from the life of God. They would experience it physically in a day to come, some years in the future.

Death and suffering are certainly negatives, and in a true sense they are evil. Yet because they are both permitted by God our loving Father, it must be because a greater good can come to us because of them. Death and suffering are part of the divine pedagogy of God; they are within His providence. They are difficult lessons, experiences hard to bear, yet they form part of His loving plan for our final good.

> Endure your trials as a form of discipline; God is treating you like sons, for what son is there who is not disciplined by his father? Everyone has shared in this

discipline, so if you do not receive it you must be illegitimate and not real sons.

After all, we had earthly fathers who disciplined us and we respected them; all the more reason, then, to be subject to the Father of spirits so we can live! For our earthly fathers disciplined us for a short time according as it seemed right to them, whereas God disciplines us for our own good so that we will be able to share in His holiness.

For the present, all discipline seems to bring grief rather than joy, but later it will yield the peaceful fruit of righteousness to those who have been trained by it.   Heb 12:7-11

Death and suffering are clearly our adversaries, yet they are for our strengthening and for our purification. Beyond these goods, death and suffering are our participation in the redeeming work of Christ. Beyond this also, there is more for us: our ultimate vocation in Christ to share in the *life* of the Trinity. This divine *life* is manifest in divine love, in charity. We find in the passion of Jesus Christ, in His holy dying, the great mystery of divine life. In the passion of Christ we find therefore the secret of life for us: it is a kenosis, self-emptying or self-giving. In dying with Christ, we *live* with Him. This is not merely the affirmation that after we die physically, we shall go to be with Him. More than this, it is that in our dying, in the graces of divine charity, we most authentically and completely are the Body of Christ. In our faithful daily sufferings and dying, we most intimately are one with Him in His glorious outpouring of love. This is our greatest joy.

Configuration to the Son's Kenosis

The central event of all history is the human life of Jesus Christ. St. Thomas, in describing a sacrament, helps us to relate sacraments to the central event of the human life of Christ: His passion. Our Catholic sacramental life places us in the presence of the passion of Christ, which is the very center of the mystery of our human existence. Therefore a sacrament is a sign that commemorates what precedes it: Christ's passion; demonstrates what is accomplished in us through Christ's passion: grace; and prefigures what that passion pledges to us: future glory.[1]

In the passion of Christ, His Sacred Heart is revealed. In the passion, the veil covering the inner life of God is torn asunder (Mt 27:51). In the passion, God reaches to the deepest depths of man's estrangement and pain, and there pours out for us His love. Mankind must come to terms with the passion of Christ. This event intrinsically demands our response. The only just and true response is our faith, our obedience, our love: in other words, our redemption and life.

Our Catholic sacramental life keeps us close to the Sacred Heart of Jesus, being touched by and touching His passion, so to speak. In this Holy Temple, we stand at the interface of human and divine life. What separates at the interface? What is the boundary for us between our present and our eternal life? There is a curtain of separation, removed in stages. The curtain is opened for us through kenosis, our dying in Christ.

The Kenosis of Christ

Have the same outlook among you that Christ Jesus had, Who, though He was in the form of God, did not consider equality with God something to hold on to. Instead, He emptied Himself and took on the form of a slave, born in human likeness, and to all appearances a man.

He humbled Himself and became obedient, even unto death, death on a cross. For this reason God highly exalted Him and gave Him a name above every other name, so that at the name of Jesus every knee shall bend, in the heavens, on earth, and below the earth, and every tongue will proclaim, to the glory of God the Father, that Jesus Christ is Lord.

Ph 2:5-11

In our liturgy of the Mass, the Church of Christ participates in the covenant in His Blood, and makes it present in the world and time. We rightly surround ourselves with sacramentals and with icons of His cross, for the cross is the emblem of His kenosis. The cross of Christ was a single event, a moment in time and human history. It was "the hour" to which He walked from the beginning of His ministry. But the cross was in a more profound sense "only" the actuality in His humanity of the essential kenosis of His Sonship. The International Theological Commission of the Church finds that Jesus' "existence for others" must be seen as "rooted in His eternal sonship."[2] In His life and death on earth which was "for" us, Jesus always did what was pleasing to the Father (CCC, 606 ff.).

The inner life of the Trinity is a great mystery — it is the greatest of all divine mysteries, "the central mystery of Christian faith and life" (CCC, 234). Yet in Jesus Christ, we begin to see the glory of God. Trinity Life reveals divine self-giving in love for the Other. The Father, who is the origin, out-pours Himself in the generation of His own Nature in love: He eternally begets the Son, who is the Word of God. The Son eternally out-pours Himself in submission to and in love for the Father. The Holy Spirit is the eternal spiration of both Father and Son: the Love, in Person, of both for the Other. The Holy Trinity has been called a *perichoresis*[3] of self-giving divine love, of kenosis.

The cross was "only" the actuality in His humanity of the eternal kenosis of the Son in love, but it was our salvation! Here at the cross, Word and Sacrament became complete for us. The oath of God in His covenant with Abram was satisfied (Gn 12:1-3); the promise of God traced back even to the proto-evangelium for the Messiah (Gn 3:15) was kept. A new humanity, in Christ, was now open. We are invited to die to our old man, through Baptism, in the death of Christ, and live to God in Christ Jesus because of His resurrection.

Christ-Encounter in Suffering

Suffering is Like a Sacrament

Suffering is like a sacrament, because it is truly an encounter with the work of the saving humanity of Jesus Christ. As with a sacrament, the benefit that the soul receives upon this encounter depends on the soul. A sacrament brings a real and special encounter with the actual Person of Christ, yet the result of that encounter depends upon the soul. For a soul who had been lost and dead, such an encounter presents the most important opportunity: that of Life itself. For a lukewarm soul, such an encounter presents again that crucial choice: the choice to remember and repent and return. For a soul warm with the Presence of Christ, such an encounter is a hard blessing: in suffering we have a taste of the bitter and the sweet cup of our vocation. Suffering will come to every person, and it need not be wasted.

Suffering recalls every sacrament, because suffering recalls the passion and hence the human suffering of Christ. Suffering recalls Baptism, our introduction and immersion into the death of Christ. Suffering recalls Confirmation, strengthening and establishing us as witnesses of His passion. Suffering recalls the Eucharist, and the brokenness of His Body, and the cup He would not take but in the will of the Father. Like the Eucharist, suffering is sacrifice completed with Communion: both our union with Him, and our union with all mankind in Him. Suffering recalls the covenant of Marriage, our conjugal union with all of fallen humanity. So also it recalls Holy Orders, the sacrament of priesthood, and reminds us of our common priesthood, ordering us with Him as priest. In suffering we are with Him as one standing between, a bridge linking mankind with God, completing His priesthood in the mystery of charity. Suffering recalls, finally, our sacrament of the Anointing of the Sick: in solidarity with all persons in all their sickness and suffering, in acceptance of all just consequences of all the sin of the world, we reach out to touch Him our healer.

Suffering enables a most intimate communion with Christ, *the* Sacrament: with the work of the saving humanity of Jesus (CCC, 774). In taking up humanity, in the sacred Incarnation, the Son became the Christ and showed us all the way out of our death through His death, and into His life. That way is the cross — His cross — the path of suffering in love. We too must take up our crosses, making up what is lacking in the sacrifice He offered. His death is the way out of the solitary death awaiting us. His death is participation in eternal life; His death is the death unto resurrection.

Scriptural Testimony

> Why is light given to the miserable,
> and life to the bitter in soul?
> Death is what they long for
> more than hidden treasure.
> They rejoice upon reaching the grave.
> Why give light to a man whose path is hidden
> and whose way God blocks at every side?
> Instead of bread I feed on sighs
> like water poured out are my groans.
> For what I fear has come upon me,
> what I dread has befallen me.
> I find no rest, I find no ease;
> only turmoil, nothing of peace!
>
> Jb 3:20-26 (CCB)

Suffering is the universal and ancient experience of mankind. Job cries out to God for all of us, for understanding of this profound dilemma: how can it be that even the innocent suffer? We can understand the suffering of the unrighteous: justice would seem to demand it. Yet it is our human experience that suffering bears no relationship to the righteousness or to the evil of persons. Suffering comes to all of us, in a measure that we cannot understand. The Psalmist cries out against the prosperity of the wicked,

> …I was envious of the arrogant,
> when I saw them prosper in their wickedness.
> For they suffer no pain;
> they are strong and sound of body,
> free from the troubles common to other men;
> they are not stricken by human ills.
>
> Ps 73:3-5 (CCB)

The writer of Ecclesiastes complains of the indifference of life toward the goodness or the evil of human persons:

> ...the same destiny awaits everyone, the virtuous and the wicked, the clean and the unclean, the one who sacrifices and the one who doesn't. It is then the same for the good man and the sinner, for the one who swears and the one who refrains from swearing.
>
> Ec 9:2 (CCB)

When Jesus walked among us and relieved suffering in the name of God, He was accepted with great joy as the hoped-for minister of God's mercy: "large crowds kept gathering to listen to Him and to be healed of their illnesses" (Lk 5:15). Yet there seemed to be a dark side to His teaching, which even His closest disciples had difficulty hearing. His good news included suffering, and the cross.

> He was teaching His disciples and telling them, "The Son of Man will be given over into the hands of men. They will put Him to death; and when He has been killed, after three days He will rise." But they could not understand what He meant, and were afraid to ask Him.
>
> Mk 9:31-32

The difficulty of His teaching was more personal than "merely" the fact that Jesus was to suffer. He promised the cross to all who would follow Him. "Whoever would be My disciple must deny himself; he must take up his cross and follow Me" (Mt 16:24). And again, "Whoever does not bear his own cross and come after Me, cannot be My disciple" (Lk 14:27). Our place with Him is indeed dependent upon our suffering with Him: "If we are children, then we are also heirs, heirs of God, co-heirs with Christ, provided we suffer with Him so as to be glorified with Him as well" (Rm 8:17).

There is, indeed, a continuing sharing in the sufferings of Christ: "If one member suffers, all the members suffer; if one member is honored, all the members rejoice" (1 Cor 12:26); "Christ's sufferings overflow and include us " (2 Cor 1:5); "If we suffer, it is for your encouragement and salvation" (2 Cor 1:6); "you share in the suffering" (2 Cor 1:7); "For God has graciously allowed you not only to believe in Christ but also to suffer for Him" (Ph 1:29); "My goal is to know Him and the power of His resurrection, to understand the fellowship of His sufferings and become conformed to His death" (Ph 3:10).

How can we understand this continued suffering, even after the one perfect sacrifice of Christ? The mysterious truth is that the cross of Christ continues in the Church, even to today. As Paul wrote, "I rejoice in what I am suffering for you now; in my flesh I am completing what is lacking in Christ's afflictions on behalf of His body, that is, the Church" (Col 1:24). Our participation in the cross of Christ, our part in the continuing redemption of humanity, is essential to the Catholic understanding of the Gospel.[4]

The saving passion of Christ is symbolized in the cup, which He struggles to accept in the Garden of Gethsemane: "And He went ahead a little and fell face down in prayer, 'My Father,' He said, 'if it is possible, let this cup pass away from Me; yet not as I wish, but as You do'" (Mt 26:39). He finds His disciples unable to keep watch with Him; they continue to fall off to sleep. Again He prays, "My Father, if it is not possible for this cup to pass by without Me drinking it, let Your will be done" (Mt 26:42). His disciples are unable to remain in prayer with Him, as they are unable to accept or even to understand the cup He must drink. But they will understand, and they will drink of it themselves (Mk 10:39). The cup of the New Covenant is to be shared by all in His kingdom: "I tell you I shall not drink again of this fruit of the vine until that day when I drink it new with you in My Father's kingdom" (Mt 26:29).

A Sacrament for the Suffering

All suffering brings with it the possibility of an encounter with Christ in His passion. The Sacrament of the Anointing brings to the suffering Christian a unique strengthening in this unique time of trial. The specific and needed effects of this sacrament are:

1. The "strengthening, peace and courage to overcome the difficulties that go with the condition."[5] Here faith is renewed, and trust in God is made stronger, even in the face of weakness and pain. This is the healing of the soul, even if God's will does not extend to the healing of the body at this time.

2. The "strength and the gift of uniting himself more closely to Christ's Passion." One who suffers is "*consecrated* to bear fruit" by becoming configured to the passion of Christ.[6] Here the Christian is greatly strengthened and encouraged as his personal pain and trial become united to His, and the passion of Christ becomes a personal invitation. The *consecration* in the suffering reveals the great value, the great potential and even the honor for the consecrated person now held in this difficult trial. The Christian is united *in his or her suffering* to the suffering Christ.

3. The gift of becoming in Christ one with Him in His self-offering for the whole Church.[7] Here the suffering of the Christian becomes one with love, even the love of God in Christ. Above, he was consecrated to bear fruit;

here the fruitfulness *in the suffering* reveals the mysterious glory and victory of the cross. Here the meaning
and value for the whole Church is revealed: the Christian is suffering, but through Christ he is suffering in
love, and for others. His suffering is meritorious.

4. The grace appropriate for preparation for the final journey of death. The *Catechism* teaches, "The Anointing
of the Sick completes our conformity to the death and
resurrection of Christ, just as Baptism began it."[8] This
most essential conformity to the death of Christ ("Whoever does not take up his cross and follow behind Me
is not worthy of Me," Mt 10:38) is made complete by
the grace of this sacrament. In the ways and graces discussed above, this conformity to His passion and death
is sacramentally accomplished. Additionally, the person
is made ready for that final step into eternity.

The Precious Death of His Holy Ones

Saint John of the Cross has written in great precision and
detail of the process of sanctification in souls God draws to Himself. In his work *The Living Flame of Love*, John extends his discussion of the purification of the soul to that final and completing act of union of the soul with God at death. John uses the
poetic image of fire to convey this holy work of the Spirit, speaking of a flame of love which God infuses into the soul of one
being drawn toward Him. In this imagery, the flame is the Spirit
of its Bridegroom, which is the Holy Spirit. The soul feels the
Holy Spirit within itself as a fire which burns and flares within
it, which has consumed and transformed it. This Spirit is experienced as bathing the soul in glory, as refreshing the soul with
divine life.

These interior acts are acts of inflamed love: the will of the soul united with these flames "loves most sublimely." Such acts of love are most precious to God, and are meritorious to the person.[9] John asserts that such a soul, so graced and so cooperative with His grace enjoys a foretaste of eternal life. Thus John understands the psalmist: "My heart and my flesh rejoiced in the living God" (Ps 83:3).

John is speaking here of a highly advanced soul in the unitive stage, deeply purified in the dark nights of purgation by the Holy Spirit. For such a soul, the experience of death is not the common one. To understand such an extraordinary encounter (as John refers to it), one must understand the encounters of the soul with God which have preceded this ultimate one.

The Death by Love

In St. John's spirituality, there are three veils which separate a soul from God: there is the veil of temporality, comprising all creatures; there is the natural veil, of natural inclinations and operations; and there is the final sensitive veil which comprises the union of the soul with the body. It is this last veil which is torn by death. The first two veils, for John, are torn when "all the things of this world are renounced, all the natural appetites and affections mortified, and the natural operations of the soul are divinized." In the soul which has attained this highest spiritual ascent, only the last veil remains: the first two have been torn in the dark nights of purgation, and the soul brought into union with Him by infused grace. Here John's understanding of the death of God's holy ones comes forward: their death is not the common one, it is the death of love.[10]

John writes:

The death of persons who have reached this state is far different in its cause and mode than the death of others, even though it is similar in natural circumstances. If the death of other people is caused by sickness or old age, the death of these persons is not so induced, in spite of their being sick or old; their soul is not wrested from them unless by some impetus and encounter of love, far more sublime than previous ones, of greater power, and more valiant, since it tears through this veil and carries off the jewel, which is the soul.[11]

These are truly remarkable statements, setting the death of the holy ones in a separate category entirely. Death is not caused by sickness or old age, John states, in the saints of God. Their death, if we would insist on keeping the same term to describe this very different event, is brought about by love and not by disintegration. It is a final act and work of love. The death of such persons is very gentle and sweet, John asserts, more so than their entire spiritual life on earth. After much purification, and expansion of the capacity of the soul for grace and charity, and intimate communion with the Holy Spirit along the spiritual journey, the holy death is not a violent taking away of soul from body. It is a most beautiful encounter with the Beloved, the completion of all those preparations in the soul. John insists, "they die with the most sublime impulses and delightful encounters of love."[12] In this way John understands the psalm: "Precious in the sight of the Lord is the death of His saints."

This radically different understanding of death for His faithful ones, offers a simple interpretation to Scripture passages in John's Gospel which otherwise are obscure. In John 8:51 we read, "Truly, truly, I say to you, if anyone keeps My word he will never see death." With the understanding of John of the

Cross, we would interpret this as saying that a soul who truly keeps the word of Christ will not experience the disintegration of sickness or old age, even if all observers of the weakening and infirm saint would believe that he was dying. The saint might indeed experience severe trial, pain, and purgation, all preparing him for that openness of soul which perfect charity requires. Through his merit, his capacity for grace and charity would be increased. But in the end, he would not die! He would never see death, as Jesus promised, but rather would experience a final encounter with love, tearing away the last veil between him and his divine Spouse.

This same possible interpretation holds for the passage (Jn 11:26), "Whoever lives and believes in Me shall never die." In the obedience of faith is a relationship, indeed a covenant, which is stronger than death. This final embrace of the soul, as John of the Cross understands the encounter, is actually formative rather than disintegrative: it is a positive act of God and not the absence of such act. John writes,

> And love is introduced as form is introduced into matter; it is done in an instant, and until then there is no act but only the dispositions toward it. Spiritual acts are produced instantaneously in the soul, because God infuses them.[13]

The trial leading up to it may be long, but the final event, the death, is quick, as the "tearing of a veil." John writes, "The enamored soul desires this tearing so that it may suffer no delay by waiting for its life to be destroyed naturally, or cut off at such and such a time." The soul begs that the veil of life be torn "immediately by a supernatural encounter and impetus of love." Hence in this sense, God perfects quickly souls who love Him ardently.[14] This encounter of love is the way John understands the passage in Wisdom:

> There was one who pleased God and was loved by Him,
>   and while living among sinners he was taken up.
>
> He was caught up lest evil change his understanding
>   or guile deceive his soul.   Ws 4:10-11

Paul the apostle clearly shared this eagerness in love to be with Christ. He wrote:

> For to me, to live is Christ, and to die is gain.
>
> If I continue to live on in the flesh, that means I will have fruitful labor; yet I do not know which to prefer.
>
> I am torn between the two alternatives — I wish to depart and be with Christ, for that is far better....
>   Ph 1:21-23

Such a soul has lived a most successful life. Making the most of the time, in the context of evil days in a contrary civilization, the person has, "through complete mortification of all the vices and appetites and of one's own nature," reached "the perfection of the spiritual life of union with God."[15] Such a person has grown through the spiritual stages of the beginner and the proficient, and has endured and traversed the dark nights of the senses and of the spirit. He has entered the stage of the perfect in Christ, and waits at the last and final door, the door of death. Here, for such a saint, only this thin veil remains.

The perfection of life, according to John of the Cross, is necessarily bound to the inherited condition of death which is due to original sin. This wisdom was expressed also by John the Evangelist, as he wrote, "We know that we have passed over from death to life because we love the brethren. Whoever does not love abides in death" (1 Jn 3:14). It is important, in understanding John of the Cross, to recognize his perspective: he considers human persons first in an inherited condition of death in the soul. He is concerned with the subsequent encounter of the soul with life. Perhaps the common view of mankind is the opposite: we presume an initial condition of life, and a coming encounter with death!

John's view of the condition of death includes all that goes to make up the old nature, the old man. Man's preoccupied engagement in the things of this world, neglecting or ignoring the supernatural realities, is death. Man's self-indulgence in appetites ordered to creaturely pleasures is all "the activity of the old life, which is the death of the new spiritual life."[16] Mankind begins in death; it is out of death that we proceed in our spiritual journey to God and to His life. The goal is to "put off the old man, your former way of life which is corrupted by deceitful desires! Be renewed in your mind and spirit, and put on the new man, created in accordance with God's design in true righteousness and holiness" (Eph 4:22-24). In such life a person truly finds perfect union with God. In its old life, all the activities of the soul were in death; in the new, in the divinity of God's life. In this divine communion, John hears repeated the words of St. Paul, "I have been crucified with Christ! It is no longer I who live; it is Christ who lives in me! And this life I live now in the flesh, I live through faith in the Son of God, who loved me and gave Himself up for me" (Gal 2:20). John explains, "The condition of death in this soul is changed to the life of God."[17]

The Question of the Death of Mary

Did Mary die? This extends the question of the death of the holy saints to its ultimate human example. Mary was free of original sin, a blessed state which places her beyond the natural condition of humankind, yet free of original sin also are baptized believers who have been forgiven all sin in Baptism and given a share in the life of the Trinity. Baptized believers who "keep" the word of Christ, remaining in His truth, have heard the promise of Jesus that they will never see death. Perhaps this promise gives us insight into Mary and her response to her vocation, as well as insight into the real meaning of a holy life.

Returning to the picture of St. John of the Cross, of the three veils which separate a soul from his Beloved and his full entry into life, we would say that Mary was not separated from God by the usual first two veils by her singular grace. She was free of the first veil, the veil of temporality, by her intrinsic contemplative openness to God. Infused contemplation in any person is a breaking through — or perhaps John would better say, a tearing — of the veil of time which obscures the timeless reality of the divine.

Through the experience of contemplation, a soul is somehow (by divine act) touched with an encounter with the eternal and absolute. In this encounter, time is judged and exposed, and stripped of the tyrannical power it had. Time is only a context, a dimension in which we have our existence yet not our essence. In the contemplative experience of God, a soul knows a certain freedom from time (though not an absolute freedom). In this experience is also a certain (though not complete) freedom from the fear of death. Death appears to rule time, to a soul imprisoned by it — but to a soul given an encounter with reality outside of time, one's own essence is better understood, and one's own vocation in the Holy Trinity is heard more clearly.

Thus the first veil, which is bound up with the first claim of death upon us, is opened with a certain freedom in contemplation. Mary, in her complete openness to God, lived an innately contemplative embrace with Him Who is outside of time: Mary was thus free of this first claim and power of death.

The second veil of which St. John of the Cross speaks is one which is torn through in the holy ones of God in much purgation, mortification, and suffering. This purgation is made necessary by our sins which have corrupted the soul even after the sanctifying grace of Baptism, and the infused virtues and gifts that He gives us with our call. The Church teaches that one who dies immediately after a sacramental Baptism would be transported directly to the presence of God: there would be nothing in the soul which God hates, at all. Our tragic yet common experience is that we do not persevere in that plenitude of grace. In the darkness of this world, our common experience is that we participate in that darkness, to the wounding and injury of our souls. Thus through much suffering, a soul cooperating with the Lord makes its return to Him. If this purgation is not completed on earth, with merit, then it is completed in purgatory, though without merit and passively. In this purgation, the second veil is torn away, and the soul is another step closer to the complete embrace he desires.

For Mary, this second veil also was not there. She remained in that purity of grace — in the very life of God — which was granted her from the beginning. Her soul was as pure and beautiful, as good, indeed "very good," as was the intention of God in the creation. Hence there was no purgation, and no tearing, as needed in the call of the saints.

What of the third veil? For St. John, this third veil is passed in the saints not by "wrenching away," as we commonly picture the violent rending of death, but rather a gentle tearing in love. The picture of St. John, with his three veils, enables us to isolate several marks of human life, and therefore to isolate conceptually the separation(s) which occur at "death." In the death of those who are godly, it seems that the effects of sin upon the soul occur certainly in the second veil, perhaps in the first, but not with the third veil. Because of the holy longing with which the saints desire this tearing of the last veil, and because this longing is that of holy and divine love, how can sin be involved? If the final veil involves the union of body with soul which is broken through love, then the union is not an essential one. Love, especially and certainly the love of God which is perfect, does not violate that which is essential. This love is calling the soul away from the body not to its annihilation or its disintegration, but rather to its integration with a body suitable to the life it now knows, the life of the Trinity.

In the model which John of the Cross presents, we can understand the "death" of Mary in this way. Her soul was not wrenched away from her in a violent sundering, which is death as most commonly understood. Her soul was called by love away, in a sweet and gentle tearing from a body which is not appropriate to resurrection life, to a resurrection-appropriate body waiting for her in the embrace of God.

How would such a "death" appear to an observer? There would be nothing violent, or violating, about it at all. In her contemplative openness, no breaking in upon her temporal being would be necessary: her door was always open to the One who comes knocking. Without stains of sin on her soul, without any ravages of sin upon her body, no force would be needed to pull her from this world, no contradiction to divine life would be found within her. But in the absence of sickness, and without the deterioration of old age, the call of the Beloved to her into the perfection of His love might resemble a swoon of love, or an ecstasy of longed-for union. Such a gentle and sweet tearing of the last veil might be spoken of as a dormition, or a lapse, outwardly speaking, into a sleep. Indeed the passing of Mary is referred to in the *Catechism* (966) as a "Dormition," quoting a prayer of the Byzantine Liturgy.

Having said all this, we must add that the majority of theologians hold that if Jesus Christ, the wholly sinless One, died a true death — was crucified, *died*, and was buried — then most probably Mary's departure from this world would have been no less a true death than His. Her death, however, is seen by them as a joyous event, a peaceful transition to glory. The Church has never officially ruled on how, when or even precisely where Mary passed from this life to the next.

Thérèse of Lisieux

Taking out of the accounts of the deaths of some of the saints, those purgations and mortifications they experienced, and the penances for charity they took upon themselves, what we can see remaining in their passing is that "death of love" that John of the Cross describes: the tearing of the last veil. Thérèse wanted that "death of love."[18] She wrote a poem as a preparation for Holy Communion, on July 12 preceding her death[19]:

> You who know my extreme littleness,
> You don't hesitate to lower Yourself to me!
> Come into my heart, O white host that I love,
> Come into my heart, for it longs for You!
> Ah, I desire that Your goodness would let me
> Die of love after receiving this favor.
> Jesus! Listen to my tender cry.
> Come into my heart!

Thérèse's actual experiences as death approached were of great suffering, both physical and spiritual, for months. She expressed a longing, however, to have that suffering, as an encouragement to other souls, to "little souls" such as herself.[20] The final tearing itself, she longed for. Her last words and movements indicated, perhaps, that the "death of love" was indeed received in the end. It was recorded on the day of her death, September 30, 1897, that she looked over to her crucifix, and said, "Oh! I love Him!..." And then, "My God!... I love you!" In appearance, her face had now regained the lily-white complexion it always had in full health. Her sister recorded: "She made certain beautiful movements with her head, as though Someone had divinely wounded her with an arrow of love, then had withdrawn the arrow to wound again." When she was looked at closely, it was seen that she had stopped breathing. It was noted that there was now a "sublime look" on her face.[21]

Francis of Assisi

Francis of Assisi had a similar experience: great suffering, yet in the end, a most sublime death. When told by a doctor of his terminal illness, Francis exclaimed: "Welcome, Sister Death!" He then called two brothers to come to his bed, to sing the Canticle to Brother Sun. As they were singing for him, Francis stopped them and added the verses[22]:

Be praised my Lord, for our Sister Bodily Death,
From whom no living man can escape.
Woe to those who die in mortal sin.
Blessed are they whom she shall find in Your
    most holy will,
For the second death shall not harm them.

The brothers sang this several times a day to comfort him, even in the night. One Brother was afraid that Francis's preparing for death with such happiness and singing would scandalize people. Francis could only reply, "Leave me be, Brother, for in spite of all that I endure, I feel so close to God that I cannot help singing."[23] This was in spite of the fact that disease had ravaged his body; it was thoroughly emaciated, a "skeleton." It was recorded, "his sufferings were atrocious." The saint's attitude was peaceful through the severe purgations leading up to the final moments: "My choice is whatever God sends me. But I must admit that the cruelest martyrdom would be easier to bear than three days of pain like this."[24] Eventually Francis died, singing. Similar to Thérèse in death, his body "was as though transformed." It was recorded that his body, long contracted through suffering, became at death supple as a child. His face appeared "beautiful as an angel's." The awesome stigmata "stood out like black stones on white marble." Brother Leo later said, "One might have thought it was the Divine Crucified, taken down from His cross, who lay there."[25]

Conclusion to the Chapter

"Whoever lives and believes in Me shall never die." This incredible promise gives us great hope on our journey, a hope grounded upon the victory of Christ over death. Fear of death is a most powerful weapon of the enemy of our souls:

> Now, since the "children" are all made of flesh and blood, He too shared in the same flesh and blood so that through His death He would destroy the one who has power over death, that is, the Devil, and in

this way would deliver those who all their lives were in bondage through fear of death. Heb 2:14-15

This passage of Scripture is most revealing. Through *fear of death*, human persons fall into a life of bondage. Due to this ultimate source of all our other unholy fears, we are subject to slavery under the power and influence of Satan! Here we see the source of our freedom in Christ: freed from this enslaving fear, we are freed from all of Satan's dominion. Freedom in Christ, freedom to truly choose *life*, is grounded in our faith in His resurrection victory over death.

A holy death is not death in the common sense of the word: it is an embrace of love. Are these mere words, or is this meaningful and absolute truth? Should one say in the end that "death is death, and don't cover it over with fancy words"? Or is there a real freedom from death to be found in this life, through the merits of Christ, available in the indwelling life of the Holy Spirit? These radical thoughts are grounded in words of Jesus that seem incredible, yet stir a most powerful hope in the soul. In the resurrection, all the redeemed will have witnessed the prophecy, "The last enemy to be destroyed is death" (1 Cor 15:26). But perhaps those few, the holy ones, who have truly fought the good fight and have taken the cup that the Father offered them, to His glory, will have conquered that enemy long before, in a final embrace of love.

Mary, and Our Dying

As Christians on our journey to God, we want a good death as we want a good life. We want not only a good final moment of death, we want also the grace of a lifetime of dying to our old nature that we might live to the new. In the lifetime moments of dying, as at the final moment of death, we are given a special help: Mary our mother. It was from His cross that Jesus gave Mary to the Beloved Disciple, and through him to all of us. As we taste the cross in faith, we too receive Mary as mother. At each moment of dying to the old nature — at each embrace of our cross on this earth — Mary is there for us, as mother, with us in our "rebirthing." Our suffering on this earth may be slight, or intense, but Mary is there. The assault of sin upon us or within us in a moment may be merely inconvenient, or tragic and terrible, but Mary is there with us and for us. Mary, our mother, is there to pray for us "now, and at the hour of our death."

The gift of Mary as mother is a most sublime treasure of our faith. It is not surprising that those separated Christians who lack a clear theology of suffering also lack a clear Mariology. Nor is it surprising that the saints and martyrs of our faith demonstrate such love and devotion to Mary. She is with us in our times of great need, those moments at the cross when we have the opportunity to enter the passion of Christ. A report comes from soldiers and sailors after war, that from many brave young men dying or near their moment of death, come cries for mother. Mary is there for us as she was there for Jesus, mother of the Body of Christ.

The whole Church prays to Mary, and looks to her intercession in a special way "now, and at the hour of our death." Each moment of our lives brings an opportunity to offer ourselves in charity to live the life of Christ on earth. We have the opportunity to offer a lifetime of dying, one moment at a time, that we may live. Thérèse and Francis, and most completely, Mary, have left examples for us of persons offering their bodies a living sacrifice. United to Christ so intimately in life, the actual moment of their death was quite unusual. Awaiting us also is a final moment, a final opportunity to offer that sacrifice, a final moment of death. A good death, for which we rightly pray, is a final embrace of God's will in faith, with hope and charity. At that moment especially, Mary will be there for us, to offer herself to mother us into the fullness of her Son.

The Antichrist

The call of Christ to His Body the Church is not without its enemies. Our vocation is to the perfection of charity, to a share in His passion, to a completion of what is lacking in His cross. The enemy of this call is the enemy of Christ, the enemy of charity, the enemy of His passion, the enemy therefore of His Church. There is a spirit against Christ, the spirit of Antichrist, which as John said even in the first century was now in the world (1 Jn 2:18). This enemy of the Lord denies the true, historical Jesus; he may or may not substitute another "Jesus" by distorting the Scripture or sacred tradition of the Church. "Who is the liar, if not whoever denies that Jesus is the Messiah? This is the Antichrist — whoever denies the Father and the Son" (1 Jn 2:22). Thus this Antichrist might overtly deny Jesus as the Christ, the Messiah, or he might simply substitute "another" Jesus, inventing a Jesus who will fit his own gospel and theology. This false gospel will, in one way or another, deny the cross and the passion for its followers. This false gospel is of and for this world.

The teaching of Antichrist may be found, even among Christians, with those who preach the distorted gospel of prosperity and success. We read of this religion at the beginning of the Church, as observed by St. Paul,

> I have told you many times, and now I tell you with
> tears in my eyes, there are many who behave like
> enemies of Christ's cross. They will end up being
> destroyed; their god is their own desires — they
> glory in their shame, their concern is for earthly
> things.   Ph 3:18-19

Such a false, materialistic gospel is the opposite of the truth of Christ: it attacks the truth of the cross, and the redemptive power of sacrificial love.

The essential message of this false gospel is that God loves you and wants the very best for you, hence He wants you to prosper and succeed in all you do. The People of God, in other words, are the winners of this world; those who are losing in life, who are the poor and needy, must not have enough faith. Those who preach this gospel present themselves as winners: they appear healthy, wealthy, good-looking, and wise. Their clothes are fashionable, the latest style with tailored fit. They are self-decorated with ornate jewelry; their hair is perfectly sculpted. They bear scant outward resemblance to a hard-working carpenter, or a rejected prophet, or a crucified Christ, or the fishermen of Galilee, or the tortured martyrs of the early Church, or the suffering and joyful saints. Can they say with Paul, "In the future let no one cause me trouble, for I bear the marks of Jesus on my body"? (Gal 6:17).

More importantly, do these teachers bear the essential inward resemblance to Christ? Do they know the peace and joy of His kenosis for the love of God? Can they confess with Paul this communion in Christ's outpouring:

> Whatever I had gained from all of this, I have come
> to consider as loss for the sake of Christ. In fact, I
> consider everything to be loss for the sake of the

surpassing greatness of knowing Christ Jesus my Lord. For His sake I have cast everything aside and regard it as so much rubbish so that I will gain Christ and be found in Him, having no righteousness of my own.   Ph 3:8-9

Our vocation is to holiness in Christ, to enter the fellowship of the Holy Trinity in Him. The gods of this world seem attractive! Money, power, pleasure, prestige, and strength, offered to fear-filled souls threatened by death, are mere bait offered to his prey. Satan crumbles, however, before Him who gave Himself in charity even unto death. Here is our salvation; here is our life: in Christ. In His life, and in His dying, we find our vocation. Our vocation is charity: the perfection of charity in Christ. "Little children, be on your guard against idols" (1 Jn 5:21).

Notes

[1] *CCC,* 1130; St. Thomas Aquinas, *Summa,* III, 60, 3.

[2] "Theology, Christology, Anthropology," *International Theological Commission: Texts and Documents,* ed. Rev. Michael Sharkey (San Francisco: Ignatius Press, 1989), 213.

[3] Meaning literally "dancing-around," an image of great joy in love and self-giving.

[4] The denial of our part in the Cross, on the other hand, is essential to the false religion of the Antichrist. This point will be further discussed later in the chapter.

[5] *CCC,* 1520.

[6] Ibid., 1521.

[7] Ibid., 1522.

[8] Ibid., 1523.

[9] Kieran Kavanaugh, O.C.D. and Otilio Rodriguez, O.C.D., *The Collected Works of St. John of the Cross* (Washington, DC: Institute of Carmelite Studies, 1979), 580.

[10] Ibid., 591.

[11] Ibid.

[12] Ibid., 592.

[13] Ibid., 593.

[14] Ibid., 594.

[15] Ibid., 607.

[16] Ibid.

[17] Ibid., 609.

[18] John Clarke, O.C.D., trans., *St. Thérèse of Lisieux, Her Last Conversations* (Washington DC: Institute of Carmelite Studies, 1977), 246.

[19] Ibid., 91.

[20] Ibid., 148.

[21] Ibid., 246.

[22] Omer Englebert, *Saint Francis of Assisi,* trans. Eve Marie Cooper (Ann Arbor, MI: Servant Books, 1979), 268.

[23] Ibid., 269.

[24] Ibid.

[25] Ibid., 274.

CHAPTER NINE

CONCLUSION

Called to Holiness

All are called to *holiness*, and to the perfection of charity. There is a *path* to take, in response to that call: as with Abraham, our father in faith, the vocation is a journey. There is an *ordinary* path to be taken: it is common, usual, normal. It is common in its full acceptance only among the saints, yet it is common to all in that it is there before us all, awaiting our acceptance. This path of the three stages is to be the normal spiritual journey — as accepted and usual as the stages of physical and emotional development of childhood, adolescence, and adulthood — the beginner, the proficient, the perfect. Said another way, these stages of spiritual growth — the purgative stage, the illuminative stage, the unitive stage — simply describe that divine norm of maturing discipleship in Christ that He Himself worked among the disciples in the beginning of the Christian era.

...in Dark Nights

The advancing stages of the soul are preceded and indeed introduced by the spiritual crisis and trial of a dark night. The two dark nights of the soul, first of the senses and later of the spirit, are well described by St. John of the Cross and have been discussed earlier in this work. It is difficult to exaggerate the value of the dark nights in spiritual growth. It is difficult to over-state the importance of accepting these trials well! The advancing stages of the soul are advancing stages in a life of grace, and of faith. In a dark night, a deeper faith is being enabled and prepared — our cooperation, and our trust, are crucial lest we weaken and turn back. We must trust God in the darkness.

Psalm 77 is quoted below in its entirety. This beautiful prayer is helpful for us in understanding the dark nights, and in receiving them well.

> I cry aloud to God —
> aloud that He may hear me.
> When in trouble I seek the Lord;
> in the night I stretch out my hand untiringly;
> my soul refusing to be consoled.   Ps 77:1-2

The soul finds itself troubled, even though it continues to look to God for help. Day and night it looks to Him, persisting faithfully, yet without consolation. This is indeed troubling. How can this be? Where is the comfort of faith?

> When I think of God, I sigh;
> when I meditate, my spirit faints.
> You keep me awake and my eyes from closing;
> I am so troubled that I cannot speak.
> I remember the days of old,

At night I consider the years of long ago,
and my spirit wonders,

"Will the Lord reject us forever?
Will He never show his favor again?
Has His steadfast love for ever vanished,
and His promise ended for all time?
Has God forgotten to be merciful?
Has He in anger withheld His compassion?"
This is what makes me distraught —
that the Most High no longer acts as before.

Ps 77:3-10

Here the trial advances, and questions trouble the soul. Will God never again come to help me? Day and night the soul continues to search for Him. Has He abandoned me forever? Has His way changed — once He was near, once He showed me His care — has He changed and turned from me?

I remember the deeds of the Lord;
yes, I recall His marvels of old.
I meditate on all Your works,
and consider Your mighty deeds.
Your way, O God, is most holy.
Is there any God greater than You, our God?
You alone are the God who works wonders,
who has displayed Your power to all.
With power You have redeemed Your people,
the sons of Jacob and Joseph.

Ps 77:11-15

Grace is given — not to take away the trial, but to remember the greatness and trustworthiness of God. The whole history

of salvation, and our own personal history of discipleship tes-
tify that God is faithful. The darkness remains darkness — the
consolations of the past do not come to comfort the soul. There
is some comfort found, however, in remembering. The soul is
strengthened, and a deeper faith is enabled.

> When the waters saw You, O God,
> they were afraid and the deep trembled.
> The clouds poured down rain;
> the skies resounded with thunder;
> Your arrows flashed from every side.
> Your thunder rolled with the whirlwind;
> Your lightning lit up the world;
> the earth shook and trembled.
> Your path led through the sea,
> Your way through the great waters;
> but Your footprints were nowhere to be seen.
> You led Your people as a flock
> by the hand of Moses and Aaron.
>
> Ps 77:16-20 (CCB)

Interior reflection within the soul, in the experience of the
trial, finds new light and understanding. The great flood was
necessary, in the sin of the days of Noah. The cleansing waters
were needed at that time, and served the purposes of God then.
So too the waters obeyed God and parted to allow Moses to walk
away from bondage and toward freedom with his people Israel.
God's way was through the waters, through the trials and purgations. The ways of our Shepherd are good; we can rest in His
hands. Even in the dark nights, we can rest in His hands.

...in Stages

We have seen the three stages of the human spiritual journey in Scripture and in Tradition, in natural and in supernatural development, in prayer and in sacred liturgy. Our path of return to God is experienced in these stages. A final layer of explanation appears to us, to make even more reasonable this way of God, when we consider the original fall into sin by Adam and Eve. That is, humanity fell from grace in three stages, a threefold disordering and separation from God. Our return to Him reverses this path, and we find restoration also in three stages. We read, in the Genesis account, "So when the woman saw that [1st stage] the tree was good for food, and that [2nd stage] it was a delight to the eyes, and that [3rd stage] the tree was desired to make one wise, she [sin and death] took of its fruit and ate; and she also gave some to her husband, and he ate" (Gn 3:6).

These three stages, by which Adam and Eve in disobedience turned away from God and toward their own spiritual death, were retraced by Christ but in obedience, when He was tempted in the desert. John the Baptist cried out in the wilderness for repentance, to make straight the way of the Lord, but in His temptation Jesus made straight the path in the wilderness for us all.

Jesus returned from the Jordan full of the Holy Spirit and was led by the Spirit through the desert for forty days while being tempted by the Devil. He ate nothing during those days; and when they were completed, He was hungry. Then the Devil said to Him, "If you are the Son of God, command this stone to become a loaf of bread."

Jesus answered him, "It is written, 'Not by bread alone shall man live.'"

Then he led Jesus up and showed Him all the kingdoms of the world in an instant of time, and the Devil said to Him, "I can give you all this power and glory; because it has been given to me and whoever I want to give it to. So, if you will worship before me, it will all be yours."

And in answer Jesus said to him, "It is written, 'The Lord your God shall you worship, and Him alone shall you serve.'"

Then he took Jesus to Jerusalem and set Him on the pinnacle of the temple, and said to Him, "If you are the Son of God, throw yourself down from here; for it is written, 'He will give His angels charge over you, to protect you,' and 'On their hands they will bear you up, lest you strike your foot against a stone.'"

In answer Jesus said to him, "It is said, 'You shall not tempt the Lord your God.'"

And when the Devil had finished all his tempting, he left Him until an opportune time.   Lk 4:1-13

We can see the correspondence of the three temptations of Jesus to the threefold temptation of Eve in Table 4 below.

Table 4	
Temptations of Eve to sin	**Temptations of Christ: Obedience**
the tree was good for food	Satan: "Command this stone to become a loaf of bread." Jesus: "It is written, 'Man shall not live by bread alone.'"
it was a delight to the eyes	Satan, showing Him his kingdoms: "I will give you all this power and glory." Jesus: "It is written, 'You shall worship the Lord your God, and Him alone shall you serve.'"
the tree was desired to make one wise	Satan to Jesus taken to Jerusalem on "the pinnacle of the temple": "Throw yourself down from here." [sin of presumption] Jesus: "It is said, 'You shall not tempt the Lord your God.'"

The threefold fall of Eve into the death of sin is not mere history that Jesus needed to revise! The threefold fall was and is present reality to all her children through the spiritual reality of original sin. Jesus chose to confront Satan on behalf of mankind again, to experience his testing and temptations again, and to reverse the fall with human and heroic obedience to God. "For just as in Adam all men die, so too in Christ they will also come to life again" (1 Cor 15:22).

Our redemption is *in Christ*, and yet our conversion *into Him* is a lifelong process, experienced in stages. We hear, from the apostle John, his warning concerning the threefold trap of this world that we who are in Christ must overcome if we are fully to share His life. The worldwide imprisonment of precious humanity in idolatry traces back to that fall in the Garden, but it remains a present reality for many and a threat to all now. We must listen and respond to the Good News given us in Christ. John writes,

> Do not love the world or what is in the world. If any one loves the world, the love of the Father is not in him, because everything *in* the world — sensual lust, covetousness, and overbearing self-confidence — is *of* the world and is not of the Father. The world is passing away as well as its desires; but whoever does the will of God will last forever.   1 Jn 2:15-17

Again we see in Table 5 below, the correspondence of these stages of temptation and threat to that of the fall in the Garden.

Table 5	
Temptations of Eve into sin	**Temptations of those "in the world" of sin**
the tree was good for food	the sensual lust of the flesh
it was a delight to the eyes	covetousness, the lust of the eyes
the tree was desired to make one wise	overbearing self-confidence, or the boastful pride of life

We see how each stage of descent into the sinful lusts of the world by all mankind after Eve and Adam, is undone by Christ and by those in Christ who ascend through the three stages of the spiritual life.

1. Sin appears "good for food" — but it is not good. In the purgative stage, the stage of the beginners, we begin conversion by turning away from sin and rather toward God and the life of grace. We strive actively to resist sin and to avoid the occasions of sin. We seek God; we intend the things of God with all the effort we can summon in His grace. The lust of the flesh can be overcome with grace through the active purgations of asceticism. We find, in Christ, that man lives by the Word of God, celebrated in the Liturgy of the Word. By His Word our hunger is satisfied, and our life is renewed.

2. Temptation and the pleasures of this life remain a "delight to the eyes;" in the illuminative stage, the light of Christ begins to deeply illuminate our lives: we begin to truly *see*. In the illuminative stage, the stage of the proficient, we advance in His life passively — with active cooperation with His grace, for He is primarily the active one here. In this stage, as on the road to Emmaus, our eyes are opened by the breaking of the bread. Our delight is now found in our perception of supernatural realities — a delight found not because of what *we* can do but because of what *He* now does in us. We see differently: we see resurrected glories. With the apostles in the Upper Room we see Him — not because of our eyes but because of His appearing — as the resurrected Christ. With Thomas we now see Jesus differently, and say with him "My Lord and my God!"

3. Still it is not finished. Our following of Christ retains our self-interest; our discipleship betrays mercenary inten-

tions. The "pride of life" — our overbearing self-confidence — remains. Entering the unitive stage, the stage of the perfect, the boastful pride of life is dealt a final blow by the hand of God upon the soul and by His grace. Humility, infused into the soul with grace, is opened to the true font of wisdom: the Holy Spirit. What is truly desired "to make one wise"? It is the Holy Spirit of God, the living water that Jesus gives. At Massah, in their wilderness trial, the house of Israel "tested God", demanding water of Him. In Christ, in the unitive stage, this deep-seated pride is extinguished, and the Church and the world begin to witness the remarkable humility of the saints. In the unitive stage of the spiritual journey, God gives the living water of His Spirit by which man will never thirst again. This is wisdom: the Spirit of God.

There is, then, an ordinary path to holiness open to those poor seeking real riches, those hungry desiring the food that endures to eternal life, those meek who fear God more than man. These most reasonable men and women are ordinary if somewhat unusual, and are normal if uncommon. These having ears to hear have heard, and have responded with a "yes". Their examples are lights in the dark sky. We need this light! The world needs holy men and women, bringing the good news of life!

ST PAULS

This book was produced by St. Pauls/Alba House, the Society of St. Paul, an international religious congregation of priests and brothers dedicated to serving the Church through the communications media.

For information regarding this and associated ministries of the Pauline Family of Congregations, write to the Vocation Director, Society of St. Paul, P.O. Box 189, 9531 Akron-Canfield Road, Canfield, Ohio 44406-0189. Phone (330) 702-0359; or E-mail: spvocationoffice@aol.com or check our internet site, www.albahouse.org